D1392989

Clinical Challenges in
WOMEN'S HEALTH

A Handbook for
Nurse Practitioners

Note: The authors and editors of this book have been careful in checking dosage recommendations and treatment schedules with standards generally accepted at the time of publication. However, as new information becomes available, changes in these recommendations may be made. The reader is advised to check with the most recent information available through the Centers for Disease Control and/or the package insert of each drug. The authors and publisher disclaim responsibility for any loss, injury, or damage resulting, directly or indirectly, from the use of and application of the content of this book.

ISBN # 0-9667890-0-8

Library of Congress Catalogue
Card # 98-068005
Printed in the United States of America

This book is dedicated to the
hard-working and committed
nurse practitioners who devote much
of their time and energy to providing
health care and to promoting wellness
in all their patients, particularly their
female patients. The devotion of
NPs to their profession has made a
major contribution to health care
in the 20th century.

Acknowledgments

The publisher and editors would like to acknowledge the contributions of the following people to the preparation of this book. Their writing, reviews, and/or suggestions played a significant role in the completion of the book.

Penelope Bosarge, MSN, CRNP
Birmingham, AL

Carolyn Buppert, JD, CRNP
Baltimore, MD

Sarah Freeman, PhD, RN, CS, CNP
Atlanta, GA

Beth Kelsey, MS, RNC, NP
Anderson, IN

Kate Driscoll Malliarakis, CNP, MSN, NCADC2
Washington, DC

Beth Moran, RN, CNP
Sag Harbor, NY

Anita Nelson, MD
California Beach, CA

Sharon Schnare, RNC, MSN, FNP, CNM
Seattle, WA

Fiona Shannon, ARNP, MPII, FNP
Kingston, WA

Carolyn Sutton, MS, RNC, WHCNP
Dallas, TX

Barbara G. Tchabovsky, BA, BS
Syosset, NY

We would like to thank our friends Jessica A. Byam
of Haddonfield, NJ, and
Karen Spencer and Victoria Baum
of Karen Spencer Design in Armonk, NY

Clinical Challenges in
WOMEN'S HEALTH

Introduction

Clinical Challenges in Women's Health: A Handbook for Nurse Practitioners is intended to provide nurse practitioners (NPs) with a quick reference guide for some common issues for women of reproductive age. It also provides nurse practitioners with some basic information concerning practice management to help those who are new to practice or who are confused by the nuances of billing, negotiating salary, and surviving in today's healthcare environment. Further, the guide provides a quick reference for common legal issues that every nurse practitioner will face in the course of practice.

The chapters on contraception and sexually transmitted diseases were chosen with the understanding that these topics, though critical to the health of young women, are often a small part of the nurse practitioner's basic curriculum. We focused a chapter on substance abuse because this topic deserves more attention than it generally receives, whether in NP curricula or in our general consideration of health promotion and disease prevention. It makes sense, given the nurse practitioner's background in prevention and skills in counseling, that information about substance abuse could be helpful in the identification and treatment of this illness.

All nurse practitioners are facing challenges in the reconfiguration of the healthcare system. To help nurse practitioners maximize their practice, this guide offers practical suggestions for billing, negotiating salaries, and keeping the NP's practice alive. The section about legal issues provides information about important issues the NP may face in daily practice.

This is by no means meant to be the complete text about providing health care to women. We hope that additional volumes of these guides will cover a myriad of additional topics, including early pregnancy care and care of the peri-menopausal and post-menopausal woman, as well as a variety of other primary care topics. We welcome suggestions.

I hope you will find this guide informative and practical. This handbook has been approved for continuing education credits by the Continuing Education Committee of the National Association of Nurse Practitioners in Reproductive Health (NANPRH). For information on how to obtain a test and CEU credits, please see the inside back cover.

I would like to thank the many contributors and reviewers of this guide as well as our publisher, NP Communications, LLC, and Wyeth-Ayerst Laboratories for providing an educational grant that has enabled us to publish this handbook for our readers.

Susan Wysocki, RNC, NP
Editor

CHAPTER 1

PATIENT EVALUATION

A complete and overall evaluation of a patient is essential for helping patients maintain wellness, for detecting suspected problems, and for appropriate interventions, referrals, and treatments. The following provides a step-by-step guide to the complete evaluation of a female patient.

Chart and History

Review Chart

For a patient you have seen before, a complete review of the patient's chart—before the patient enters your office—is appropriate. Check when the patient last visited you and if there are any ongoing problems or treatments. A check on the patient's age may also suggest some specific concerns you may want to address. Such a review will help you re-establish rapport with the patient and direct some of your specific questioning.

For a new patient, you will probably have your office assistant or secretary have the patient fill out a form with identifying information. Be sure to read it over carefully before starting to talk with or examine the patient.

Identifying Statement

The patient's statement for the chart should include the following information:

>   Date
>   Date of Birth
>   Birthplace
>   Race
>   Marital Status
>   Education

Occupation
Living Environment
Financial Status
Religion
Relationships
Past History
Current Health Status
Source of Referral - helps understand motivation
Source of History - helps assess bias and
    reliability of data

Patient Profile
Besides the above identifying information, additional
information will help you develop an overall profile of
the patient and her life. If a patient does not complete
answers to some questions, you may wish to consider
gentle probing for answers in your initial interview.
Among the topics that a patient profile may include are
the following:

Life Goals
Life Changes
Allergies
Sexual Orientation/Concerns about Sexuality
Environmental Hazards
Fears—of sexual or physical abuse; of partner;
    of domestic situations
Development Tools
Coping Strategies
Medications
Resources and Supports - Relationships
Exposure to Toxins: Use of alcohol, tobacco,
    marijuana, and other drugs
Exercise/Leisure Activities
Sleep/Rest
Sense of Control of Health
Level of Stress
Stress Management
Level of Wellness

Physical Evaluation

Patient History
>Medical
>Surgical
>Obstetrical/Gynecological
>Sexual

Family History

Chief Concern: Why is client seeing you?

History of Present Illness: Ask the patient questions such as

- When did symptoms begin?

- What are the symptoms?

- What is the duration, severity, quantity, quality, and timing of the symptoms?

- What appears to have precipitated the start of the symptoms? Or what appears to precipitate isolated episodes of symptoms?

- Has any major life event occurred in your life recently (e.g., death of a spouse or loved one, divorce, children leaving home)?

- Is any laboratory data available? Or should specific lab tests be ordered?

- What do you (the patient) think is going on?

- What led you to seek attention?

Review of Systems (ROS)—general, skin, head, eyes, ears, nose, sinuses, mouth, throat, neck, breasts, respiratory, cardiac, gastrointestinal, gynecological, musculo-skeletal, neurologic.

Remember a cardinal rule:
Listen to the patient.
She will give you the diagnosis.

Physical Examination

General Observation: skin, lesions, color, hair, and nails

Vital Signs: blood pressure, pulse, respiratory rate

Height and Weight

Head Region

Inspect head region and palpate as necessary.

face, hair, and scalp;

eyes - sclera, conjunctiva, pupils;

ears - external, auditory acuity, auricles, canals, drums;

nose - external, nasal mucosa and septum, turbinates, tenderness of maxillary and frontal sinuses;

throat and mouth - lips, teeth, gums, oropharynx, tongue;

lymph nodes - preauricular, postauricular, occipital, tonsillar, parotid, submaxillary, submental, cervical, and supraclavicular.

Thyroid - Palpate for size and presence of masses.

Lungs - Listen for breath sounds - anterior and posterior auscultation.

Back - Check for scoliosis.

Kidneys - Check costal vertebral angle (CVA) for tenderness.

Heart - Determine if normal sinus rhythm is present.

Breasts

Palpate carefully and inspect entire breast, including nipple.

Express nipple.

Palpate axilla.

Palpate lymph nodes - supraclavicular, subclavian, brachial, scapular, intermediate, mammary, and internal mammary.

Abdomen

Inspect and palpate all four quadrants superficially and deeply.

Palpate liver and spleen.

> ### *If patient is pregnant:*
>
> Measure fundal height, using tape measure extending from suprapubic bone to top of fundus.
>
> Palpate uterus, using Leopold four-step method, to determine position and presentation of the fetus in late second and in third trimester.
>
> Listen to fetal heart sounds.

Lower Extremities
> Inspect and check range of motion.
> Look for Homan's sign.

Peripheral Vascular
> Check for varicose veins and/or edema.

Neurologic
> Observe gait.
> Check arm strength and grip and reflexes.

Mental Status - Does patient seem disoriented?

Gynecological Examination - The following is a detailed step-by-step approach to the examination of the female genital region.

> *External Genitalia*
> > Adust light and stool.
> > Put glove on examining hand.
> > Let client know you are going to touch her by touching her inner thigh gently and announcing that you are beginning the exam.
> > Inspect external genitalia.
> > Milk skene glands.
> > Palpate Bartholin glands.
> > Assess muscle - ask client to bear down to check for cystocele or rectocele.
>
> *Speculum Examination*
> > Take a plastic disposable or warm metal speculum.
> > Insert it gently while holding labia open.
> > Locate the cervix and examine.

Perform Pap and STD testing as appropriate.
Rotate speculum and inspect the entire vagina.

Bimanual Examination:
Separate labia.
Lubricate fingers - index and third - and insert with palm down.
Palpate all of vagina.
Note character of cervix - firm or soft, painful or tender.
Move in four directions.
Place fingers anterior and posterior to cervix to locate uterus.
Divide fingers into a V and walk up the sides to palpate the size of uterus.
Determine position of the uterus — anteverted, retroverted, or midline.
Palpate adnexa bilaterally.

Recto-Vaginal Examination
Change gloves - ask permission.
Tell patient to bear down.
Insert middle finger into rectum.
Insert index finger into vagina and rotate wrist upward.
Palpate rectovaginal septum.
Palpate cul de sac.
Confirm bimanual findings.
Palpate uterine sacral ligaments.
Remove index finger 2 inches and ask client to contract sphincter.
Palpate rectum for any masses.

Remember...
Talk with the patient during the gyn exam and observe her face for any sign of discomfort.

This chapter was prepared by Beth Moran, RN, CNP, who has an independent integrated women's health practice in Sag Harbor, New York.

CHAPTER 2

CONTRACEPTION, WITH AN EMPHASIS ON ORAL CONTRACEPTIVES

The availability of effective methods of contraception can make a significant impact on the health and lives of women and their families. However, it should be noted that currently in the United States more than half of achieved pregnancies are unintended. In choosing a method of contraception, consider the following factors:

- A woman's ability to become pregnant spans over four decades. Contraceptive needs and preferences change over time. What is suitable for a woman at one time in her life may not be suitable at another time.

- Contraceptive decisions are more complex than they may appear. Decisions involve issues that may not be immediately apparent, including religious issues, partner issues, ambivalence about pregnancy and/or sex, family issues, etc.

- For many women, the ability to become pregnant in the future is as important as the prevention of pregnancy is in the present.

- With the exception of absolute contraindications for a particular method, contraceptive choice should be the woman's.

- The more choices a woman is given, the more likely she will be to find the method that suits her needs and the more likely she will be successful in achieving her fertility goals.

Provide referrals for methods that you do not provide.

- Women have a right to change their choice of contraceptive at any time.

- Flexibility by clinicians can enhance a woman's success with contraception—for example, providing oral contraceptives to a healthy woman with a negative history before she has her annual physical.

- A thorough history is the most important aspect of providing hormonal contraception. Pap smears are important for reproductive age women, but they are not related to the initiation of hormonal contraception.

- Counseling and education are keys to successful use of contraception. Repetition of information, simple written instructions, and inquiries about use at follow-up visits are a few strategies that can increase correct use.

- Contraceptives are only as effective as the consistency and correctness with which they are used.

- The effectiveness of a specific contraceptive method differs with different patient populations. Factors such as frequency of intercourse, a couple's inherent fertility, and age affect the risk for pregnancy.

- Neither people nor methods of contraception are perfect. Anticipate the possible need for emergency contraception and provide information, and perhaps even supplies, for unanticipated events.

- With the exception of condoms, contraceptive methods do not provide protection against sexually transmitted diseases (STDs), including

HIV. Ask about risks for STDs. For those sexually active patients at risk, consider condoms as the first-line defense against STDs and a second method, such as oral contraceptives, as the extra insurance against pregnancy. Patients should also be aware that having multiple partners increases their risk of acquiring an STD.

Characteristics of Different Methods of Contraception

The contraceptive methods available to women differ in a number of characteristics. Discussion of these characteristics can help a woman find a method that most suits her needs.

Important factors to consider in the choice of a contraceptive method are outlined in the following pages.

Combined Oral Contraceptives (COCs)

Frequency of Decision to Use: Daily

Coitus Linked: No

Partner Involvement Required: None

Protection Against STDs/HIV: None

Prescription Required: Yes

Need for Healthcare System Contact to Start: Yes

Need for Healthcare System Contact to Stop: No

Systemic Effects: Yes

Noncontraceptive Benefits: Decreased problems associated with the menstrual cycle, such as pain at ovulation, cramps, heavy bleeding, PMS, and menstrual headaches; decreased anemia; decreased acne and hirsutism; decreased benign breast disease; preservation of fertility by decreased incidence of PID and ectopic pregnancy; prevention of ovarian and endometrial cancer, especially with longer duration of use; improvement of rheumatoid arthritis; and possible decreased risk of osteoporosis

OC Myth

Myth	Fact
The pill causes cancer.	Birth control pills significantly reduce the risk of ovarian and endometrial cancer. The longer a woman uses them, the greater the protection. The risk of breast cancer has not been found to increase in the long run.

■　■　■　■

Myth	Fact
The pill causes infertility.	Birth control pills prevent pregnancy when they are being taken daily, but there is a rapid return of fertility after the pills are stopped. Decreased incidence of PID and ectopic pregnancy associated with use of the pill means preserved fertility for women on the pill.

■　■　■　■

Myth	Fact
A woman should wait 3 months after stopping birth control pills before she tries to become pregnant.	Women should have their last pill-induced menses and one spontaneous menses before conception if possible. If a woman becomes pregnant on her first pill-free cycle, her last menstrual period (LMP) may not accurately reflect gestational age. If the uterus is small, ultrasound can determine gestational age.

This myth is particularly dangerous not only because of the negative image it creates of the pill, but also because it suggests that there is some lingering contraceptive effect of the pill which persists after a woman stops taking her oral contraceptives.

Busters

Myth	Fact
Women need to give their bodies a rest from the pill ...every 3 years?...every 5 years?	The only side effect which increases with duration of use is amenorrhea. When women stop the pill, they not only increase their risk of pregnancy but they also lose noncontraceptive benefits of the pill.

■ ■ ■ ■

The pill makes women gain weight.	In multiple controlled studies, women on modern oral contraceptives have not shown weight gain attributable to the pill. Women tend to gain weight over time whether or not they are taking OCs.

■ ■ ■ ■

Teenagers who smoke cannot use the pill.	Teenagers should not smoke. All women should stop smoking before they become pregnant. Birth control pill use in adolescent smokers does not pose a significant health hazard but does prevent more serious problems such as teen pregnancy.

■ ■ ■ ■

Women over 35 should not take the pill.	Only women over 35 who smoke or who have certain medical conditions should not take the pill.

Contraindications: Previous history of stroke, myocardial infarction (MI), venous thromboembolism or risk for venous embolism; hypertension 160+/100+mm Hg or presence of vascular disease; history of breast cancer; vaginal bleeding of unknown origin; pregnancy; gallbladder disease; age over 35 if a smoker; and uninvestigated family history of thrombotic disorders in young relatives. In addition, use of rifampicin, griseofulvin, phenytoin, ethotoin, mephenytoin, carbamazepine, phenobarbital, topriramate, and primidone may decrease the efficacy of oral contraceptives and may cause breakthrough bleeding. COCs are not the method of choice during lactation or within 21 days postpartum, but they can be used at the clinician's discretion.

Disadvantages: May cause annoying side effects such as nausea, breast tenderness, breakthrough bleeding and spotting, or a change in mood or sex drive (decrease or increase). There is no evidence that COCs cause weight gain beyond weight fluctuations that are experienced by women not using COCs. Preexisting sub-fertility will be unchanged after pills are discontinued.

Return to Fertility After Discontinuing Use: Can be almost immediate

Use When Lactating: May decrease quantity of breast milk

Privacy: Requires supplies

Education Points: COCs must be taken correctly and consistently to be effective. Review instructions for use and advise patients when they should seek consultation with a clinician.

Progestin-Only Pills – Mini-Pills

Frequency of Decision to Use: Daily
Coitus Linked: No
Partner Involvement Required: None
Protection Against STDs/HIV: None
Prescription Required: Yes

Need for Healthcare System Contact to Start: Yes

Need for Healthcare System Contact to Stop: No

Systemic Effects: Yes

Noncontraceptive Benefits: Decreased menstrual flow, cramps, and pain with ovulation and less anemia. Given that cessation of ovulation is thought to be the reason for a decreased risk of endometrial cancer, ovarian cancer, PID, and ectopic pregnancy with COCs, it is reasonable that progestin-only pills may also have these same benefits for those patients who do not ovulate or who ovulate less often. However, specific data on these possible benefits are lacking.

Contraindications: Precautions in the package insert are similar to those for combined pills; however, progestin-only pills contain no estrogen so some of the warnings have not been proven to be valid or invalid. Contraindications are similar to those for COCs and include breast cancer, pregnancy, cardiovascular disease or history thereof, unexplained vaginal bleeding, and liver disease. Because of decreased contraceptive efficacy, women using the medications listed for combined oral contraceptives should also avoid use of the progestin-only pill.

Disadvantages: Must be taken absolutely correctly. Progestin-only pills have a much lower margin of error than combined pills. A backup method must be used if pills are taken 3 hours late. Progestin-only pills may cause disruption of bleeding patterns, including breakthrough bleeding, spotting, or amenorrhea.

Return to Fertility After Discontinuing Use: Rapid

Use When Lactating: Yes, once lactation is established

Privacy: Requires supplies

Education Points: As with COCs, progestin-only pills must be taken on time, every day. Advise patients to report promptly abdominal pain (ovarian cyst or ectopic pregnancy); delayed period, especially if periods have been regular; repeated or very severe headaches or blurred vision. Progestin-only pills must be started on the first day of menses.

Comparative Effectiveness of Different Methods of Contraception*

Percentage of women in the United States experiencing an unintended pregnancy during the first year of typical use of contraception and the percentage continuing use at the end of the first year

Method	% of Women Experiencing an Unintended Pregnancy within the First Year of Use		% of Women Continuing Use at One Year
	Typical Use[1]	Perfect Use[2]	
Chance[3]	85	85	
Spermicides (e.g. foams, creams, gels, vaginal suppositories	26	6	40
Periodic Abstinence[4]	25		63
Calendar		9	
Ovulation Method (cervical mucus)		3	
Symptothermal (ovulation (ovulation + calendar+ basal body temperature)		2	
Post-ovulation		1	
Cap			
Parous Women	40	26	42
Nulliparous Women	20	9	56
Diaphragm	20	6	56
Withdrawal	19	4	
Condom			
Female Reality	21	5	56
Male	14	3	61
Pill	5		71
Progestin only		0.5	
Combined		0.1	
IUD			
Progesterone T	2.0	1.5	81
Copper T 380A	0.8	0.6	78
Depo-Provera	0.3	0.3	70
Norplant System®	0.05	0.05	88
Female Sterilization	0.5	0.5	100
Male Sterilization	0.15	0.10	100

1. Among typical couples who use a method, the percentage who experience an accidental pregnancy during the first year if they do not stop use for any reason.

2. Among couples who use a method consistently and correctly, the percentage who will experience an accidental pregnancy during the first year if they do not stop use for any other reason.

3. The percentages given here are based on data from populations that do not use contraception and from women who cease contraception in order to become pregnant, adjusted to represent the percentages who would likely become pregnant within 1 year among women now relying on reliable methods of contraception if they abandoned contraception altogether.

4. The percentages of accidental pregnancy differ with perfect use of the different methods used to determine the times for periodic abstinence.

*Hatcher R, et al. Contraceptive Technology, 17th ed. New York: Irvington Press 1998.

Progestin-Only Implants – The Norplant System®

Frequency of Decision to Use: Every 5 years

Coitus Linked: No

Partner Involvement Required: None

Protection Against STDs/HIV: None

Prescription Required: Yes

Need for Healthcare System Contact to Start: Yes

Need for Healthcare System Contact to Stop: Yes

Systemic Effects: Yes

Noncontraceptive Benefits: Long-term use—up to 5 years—is associated with the same benefits as the progestin-only pills.

Contraindications: Same as with progestin-only pills. Note drugs that may decrease effectiveness.

Disadvantages: Frequently causes disruption of bleeding patterns, particularly during the first year of use. Requires skilled clinician to insert and remove. May leave small scar at point of insertion and removal. Implant site may show implants or darkening of skin over the implant site. There may be an increased risk of ovarian cysts.

Return to Fertility After Discontinuing Use: Immediate

Use When Lactating: Yes, once lactation is established

Privacy: May be seen in arm

Education Points: Although good levels of the hormone are seen within 24 hours, it may be prudent to advise the patient to use a back-up method of contraception for 1 week if implant was inserted after the 5th day of the start of menses. Advise patient of cautionary signs—which are the same as those for progestin-only pills. In addition, patients should be told to report arm pain and any signs of infection at the insertion site and/or signs of implant expulsion. Provider should remind patient about removal/reinsertion date.

Progestin Injections – Depo-Provera

Frequency of Decision to Use: Every 3 months

Coitus Linked: No

Partner Involvement Required: None

Protection Against STDs/HIV: None

Prescription Required: Yes

Need for Healthcare System Contact to Start: Yes

Need for Healthcare System Contact to Stop: No

Systemic Effects: Yes

Noncontraceptive Benefits: Effective for women taking medications that decrease the efficacy of combined oral contraceptive pills and for women using other progestin-only methods. Injections decrease the frequency of seizures and provide other health benefits associated with progestin-only methods.

Contraindications: Same as those with other progestin-only methods, with the exception that the only drug that may decrease the effectiveness of Depo-Provera is aminoglutethimide (Cytadren) used to treat Cushing's Syndrome. Fear of injections is also a contraindication.

Disadvantages: Not appropriate for women who may want to become pregnant in the next 1 1/2 years since fertility return is delayed for 6-12 months. Frequently causes disruption of bleeding patterns, most frequently amenorrhea after prolonged use (although some women may consider this advantageous). Bloating, depression, and breast tenderness may also occur. Weight gain is reported in the package insert but is not experienced by all women. (No studies on weight gain have been conducted in women in the United States; one small study of women in Europe reported very small increases.) Possible short-term effects on bone density are being studied. Use may result in adverse lipid changes—a decrease in high-density lipoprotein (HDL) cholesterol—but the clinical significance of these changes is not known. Allergic reactions are rare.

Return to Fertility After Discontinuing Use: Average delay of 6-12 months

Use When Lactating: Yes, once lactation has been established. The injections may increase quantity of breast milk.

Privacy: Yes

Education Points: Although good levels of the hormone are seen within 24 hours, it may be prudent to advise use of a back-up method for one week if first injection is after the 5th day of the start of menses. Return for injections within 12 weeks. Injections may be given earlier, if more convenient to a woman's schedule. Advise patient about cautionary signs, which are the same as those for the progestin-only pill, plus lasting pain or signs of infection at the injection site.

Diaphragm

Frequency of Decision to Use: Longest wear–24 hrs, additional spermicide with every act of intercourse without removal of diaphragm; duration of protection after insertion–6 hours

Coitus Linked: Yes

Partner Involvement Required: None

Protection Against STDs/HIV: If not used multiple times in one day may decrease risk of HIV; but if used frequently in a short interval of time may increase risk of HIV (due to abrasions). Condoms or abstinence continue to be the safer alternatives for women who have their partner's cooperation.

Prescription Required: Yes

Need for Healthcare System Contact to Start: Yes

Need for Healthcare System Contact to Stop: No

Systemic Effects: No

Noncontraceptive Benefits: Use with spermicide adds vaginal lubrication. Spermicide may also act as a microbicide, possibly decreasing risk of an STD. The diaphragm may decrease or increase risk of HIV, depending on the presence of microlesions in the vaginal cavity resulting from mechanical action of the device and/or through use of the spermicide.

Contraindications: Allergy to latex or spermicide in woman or partner

Disadvantages: Can change environment of vagina, increasing frequency of some vaginal infections and UTIs. May cause mechanical irritation to the vagina or cervix or to the partner. Risk of toxic shock syndrome (TSS), rare. It may be felt by partner.

Return to Fertility After Discontinuing Use: Immediate

Use When Lactating: Yes

Privacy: Requires supplies

Education Points: Add spermicide with repeated acts of intercourse. Do not remove the device or douche before 6 hours after last intercourse. Avoid use of petroleum-based products and oils, including some vaginal medications, since these products will damage latex. A diaphragm needs to be refitted after pregnancy.

Cervical Cap

Frequency of Decision to Use: Longest wear–48 hrs; spermicide used once at insertion

Coitus Linked: No

Partner Involvement Required: None

Protection Against STDs/HIV: Similar to that for diaphragm.

Prescription Required: Yes

Need for Healthcare System Contact to Start: Yes

Need for Healthcare System Contact to Stop: No

Systemic Effects: No

Noncontraceptive Benefits: Use with spermicide adds vaginal lubrication and may decrease risk of STD. (See benefits listed under Diaphragm.)

Contraindications: Allergy to latex or spermicide in woman or partner

Disadvantages: Can change environment of vagina increasing frequency of some vaginal infections and UTIs. May cause mechanical irritation to the vagina or cervix or to the partner. Risk of toxic shock syndrome (TSS), rare. Cap may be felt by partner.

Return to Fertility After Discontinuing Use: Immediate

Use When Lactating: Yes

Privacy: Requires supplies

Education Points: Add spermicide at time of insertion. Use of cap not recommended with menses. Do not remove the device or douche before 6 hours after last intercourse. Use of petroleum-based products and oils, including some vaginal medications, should be avoided since these products will damage latex.

Postcoital Methods

Frequency of Decision to Use: For emergency use after coitus

Coitus Linked: No

Partner Involvement Required: None

Protection Against STDs/HIV: None

Prescription Required: Yes

Need for Healthcare System Contact to Start: Yes

Need for Healthcare System Contact to Stop: No

Systemic Effects: Yes

Disadvantages: Not for use as regular contraception given its side effects and its failure rate that is significantly higher than that with combined oral contraceptives

Return to Fertility After Discontinuing Use: Rapid

Use When Lactating: Only progestin-only pills or IUD

Privacy: Yes

See Emergency Contraception on page 46.

Male Latex Condoms

Frequency of Decision to Use: Every coitus

Coitus Linked: Yes

Partner Involvement Required: Yes

Protection Against STDs/HIV: Yes

Prescription Required: No

Need for Healthcare System Contact to Start: No

Need for Healthcare System Contact to Stop: No

Systemic Effects: No

Noncontraceptive Benefits: Next to abstinence, best protection against sexually transmitted diseases (STDs)

Contraindications: Latex allergy (polyurethane condoms are marketed)

Disadvantages: May cause skin irritation and may interrupt sexual foreplay. The male partner may perceive decreased sexual arousement, but this is unproven.

Return to Fertility After Discontinuing Use: Immediate

Use When Lactating: Yes

Privacy: No

Education Points: Use with a vaginal spermicide increases effectiveness. Correct use includes placing the condom on the penis before any penetration and removing it before erection decreases. Oil-based lubricants, including petroleum jelly, lotions, and oils, and some vaginal medications destroy latex. Use only water-soluble products or saliva for lubrication. Air should be pinched out of the reservoir when the condom is placed on the penis.

Female Condoms

Frequency of Decision to Use: Every coitus

Coitus Linked: Yes

Partner Involvement Required: Some

Protection Against STDs/HIV: Yes

Prescription Required: No

Need for Healthcare System Contact to Start: No

Need for Healthcare System Contact to Stop: No

Systemic Effects: No

Noncontraceptive Benefit: Only female barrier method to prevent STDs, including HIV

Contraindications: None (Made of polyurethane, not latex, so can be used by those with latex allergy)

Disadvantages: Awkward to use for some. Spillage of semen can occur if it is not removed immediately or correctly.

Return to Fertility After Discontinuing Use: Immediate

Use When Lactating: Yes

Privacy: No

Education Points: Insert prior to penile penetration; may be placed up to 8 hours before intercourse. Place inside ring in the vagina; outside ring must be out of the vagina. Do not allow outside ring to be pushed into vagina during intercourse. Remove immediately after intercourse before standing up. Squeeze and twist outer ring to keep semen inside. Do not reuse; a new female condom must be used with each act of intercourse.

Vaginal Spermicide

Frequency of Decision to Use: Every coitus

Coitus Linked: Yes

Partner Involvement Required: None

Protection Against STDs/HIV: If not used multiple times in one day may decrease risk of HIV, but if used frequently in a short interval of time may increase risk of HIV (due to abrasions). Therefore, condoms or abstinence continue to be safer alternatives for women who have their partner's cooperation. Spermicide does decrease risk of other STDs.

Prescription Required: No

Need for Healthcare System Contact to Start: No

Need for Healthcare System Contact to Stop: No

Systemic Effects: No

Noncontraceptive Benefits: Adds vaginal lubrication and may decrease risk of HIV and other STDs

Contraindications: Allergic reaction in either partner

Disadvantages: May change vaginal environment and increase frequency of vaginal or urinary tract infections

Return to Fertility After Discontinuing Use: Immediate

Use When Lactating: Yes

Privacy: Supplies required

Education Points: Increased efficacy when used with other barrier method. Must be used with every act of intercourse. Douching before 6 hours after last use with intercourse is contraindicated.

Intrauterine Device (IUD) – Copper T IUD – Paragard-T®

Frequency of Decision to Use: Every 10 years

Coitus Linked: No

Partner Involvement Required: No

Protection Against STDs/HIV: None

Prescription Required: Yes

Need for Healthcare System Contact to Start: Yes

Need for Healthcare System Contact to Stop: Yes

Systemic Effects: Limited to reproductive tract

Noncontraceptive Benefits: None

Contraindications: Active or recent (within 3 months) infection of the reproductive tract; presence of STD or risk thereof; uterine or cervical abnormalities that would prevent proper placement; pregnancy; undiagnosed abnormal vaginal bleeding; allergy to copper or Paragard-T®.

Disadvantages: Dysmenorrhea or increased bleeding. The device should not be used in women in whom

Progestasert System, a different type of IUD, provides improvements in dysmenorrhea and menorrhagia for many women. The duration of use for this IUD is one year.

the presence of a cervical STD at insertion can not be ruled out.

Return to Fertility After Discontinuing Use: Rapid

Use When Lactating: Yes

Privacy: String may be felt by partner.

Education Points: Teach patient how to check for the string to ensure proper placement. Advise about signs to report, including abdominal pain or pain with intercourse; unusual bleeding, spotting, or discharge; a missed period; systemic signs of infection such as fever, chills, or malaise; and a missing string or a string that is shorter or longer than usual. Advise patient to consider another method if she is at risk for a STD.

Fertility Awareness Methods

Frequency of Decision to Use: Initially requires daily charting

Coitus Linked: No, but requires periodic abstinence

Partner Involvement Required: Yes

Protection Against STDs/HIV: None

Prescription Required: No

Need for Healthcare System Contact to Start: Yes, for teaching

Need for Healthcare System Contact to Stop: No

Systemic Effects: No

Return to Fertility After Discontinuing Use: Immediate

Use When Lactating: Not reliable

Privacy: Yes, but requires partner cooperation

Education Points: Patient needs detailed instructions on the specific method being used.

Lactational Amenorrhea Method

Frequency of Decision to Use: Constant. Requires full breast-feeding around the clock with no supplemental bottle-feeding. Amenorrhea must be present. Method should be used no more than 3 months post-partum for maximum effectiveness.

Coitus Linked: No

Partner Involvement Required: No

Protection Against STDs/HIV: None

Prescription Required: No

Need for Healthcare System Contact to Start: No

Need for Healthcare System Contact to Stop: No

Systemic Effects: No

Return to Fertility After Discontinuing Use: Rapid

Privacy: Yes

Education Points: Advise woman of the need for full breast-feeding without supplementation and to use another form of contraception immediately after any bleeding returns.

Withdrawal

Frequency of Decision to Use: Every coitus

Coitus Linked: Yes

Partner Involvement Required: Yes

Protection Against STDs/HIV: Unknown

Prescription Required: No

Need for Healthcare System Contact to Start: No

Need for Healthcare System Contact to Stop: No

Systemic Effects: No

Noncontraceptive Benefits: Requires no supplies.

Contraindications: Counters sexual urge

Disadvantages: Low efficacy. Preejaculatory semen may contain HIV in infected men. Preejaculatory semen, particularly with subsequent intercourse, can contain sperm.

Return to Fertility After Discontinuing Use: Immediate

Use When Lactating: Yes

Privacy: Requires partner cooperation

Education Points: Better than no method. Correct use essential. Ejaculate should be kept away from vaginal opening.

Female Sterilization

Frequency of Decision to Use: One decision

Coitus Linked: No

Partner Involvement Required: No

Protection Against STDs/HIV: None

Prescription Required: No

Need for Healthcare System Contact to Start: Yes

Need for Healthcare System Contact to Stop: Yes

Systemic Effects: No

Noncontraceptive Benefits: Permanent, one-time decision

Contraindications: Unsure of making permanent decision

Disadvantages: Associated with more morbidity and mortality than male sterilization. Reversal is expensive and only moderately successful. Reversal chances are approximately 60% but vary depending on the surgical method used.

Return to Fertility After Discontinuing Use: N/A

Use When Lactating: Yes

Privacy: Yes

Education Points: Consider a consult with a professional counselor for women with factors that have been associated with high rates of requests for reversal; such factors include age under 25 and recent termination of a relationship. Advise the patient to consider the procedure irreversible. Advise about other methods, especially long-term methods. Consider other methods if unsure. Provide post-op instructions. Explain to the patient the possibility of the rare risk of ectopic pregnancy.

Male Sterilization

Frequency of Decision to Use: One decision

Coitus Linked: No

Partner Involvement Required: No

Protection Against STDs/HIV: None

Prescription Required: No

Need for Healthcare System Contact to Start: Yes

Need for Healthcare System Contact to Stop: Yes

Systemic Effects: No

Noncontraceptive Benefits: Permanent, one-time decision; simpler than female procedure

Contraindications: Unsure of making permanent decision

Disadvantages: Chances for reversal are approximately 70% but vary from 20% to 80% depending on the procedure and the length of time since the procedure.

Return to Fertility After Discontinuing Use: N/A

Use When Lactating: Yes

Privacy: Yes

Education Points: Consider as irreversible. Advise about other methods, especially long-term methods. Advise that procedure is not effective immediately. Another method of contraception should be used until sperm count confirms that procedure has been effective.

Some General Considerations Concerning Oral Contraceptives

Oral contraceptives (OCs) are a popular, easy-to-use method of contraception for many women. For these women, the advantages of this method of birth control and its noncontraceptive benefits outweigh any negative effects. For some women, however, oral contraceptives are contraindicated, and for others, the side effects and their management must be clearly understood.

Contraindications

Oral contraceptives are contraindicated for women who:

- have a history of heart attack or stroke;

- have thromboembolic disease or have a family history of young relatives with thrombotic disorders;
- are known to have or are suspected of having breast cancer;
- have active liver disease or impaired liver function;
- have vaginal bleeding of unknown origin;
- may be pregnant;
- are over 35 years of age and smoke.

All other contraindications are relative and should be weighed against the risks of pregnancy and the acceptability of other methods of contraception. For example, the woman with uncomplicated diabetes may be a candidate for the pill, as she is particularly in need of an effective method of contraception since pregnancy may have a profound effect on the regulation of her disease. (This is not to imply that a woman with diabetes cannot have a healthy pregnancy, but the pregnancy should be carefully planned and monitored.) Other women, such as women with menstrual migraines, may benefit from the pill's frequent noncontraceptive effect of alleviating cyclic headaches.

When clinicians prescribe COCs to women with ongoing medical problems, such as diabetes, it is prudent to consult with the woman's primary care provider/specialist.

Women with a family history of relatives with thromboembolic disease at a young age should be evaluated for inherited defects of coagulation (specifically Factor V Leiden) that may place them at greater risk for thromboembolic events.

Choosing an Oral Contraceptive
Except in rare circumstances, choose a low-dose (sub-50mcg) pill. Most women will do well on the first OC prescribed.

FACTORS TO CONSIDER WHEN SELECTING A HORMONAL CONTRACEPTIVE

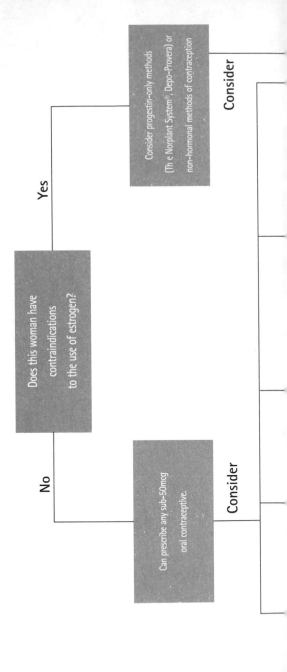

Does this woman have contraindications to the use of estrogen?

No

Yes

Can prescribe any sub-50mcg oral contraceptive.

Consider progestin-only methods (The Norplant System®, Depo-Provera) or non-hormonal methods of contraception

Consider

Consider

Has this woman had nausea, breast tenderness, or vascular headaches?

If using the lowest dose estrogen desirable due to patient preference, age, or other reason?

Has the woman experienced breakthrough bleeding or spotting while using her current OC?

Yes

Does the woman desire improvement of acne, oily skin, or hirsutism?

Yes

Is the woman taking medications, such as rifampicin, griseofulvin, phenytoin, phenobarbital, carbamazepine, topirnate, or primadone, that might decrease oral contraceptive or Norplant System® efficacy?

Yes

Yes

Prescribe a 20mcg pill (Alesse or Loestrin 1/20). While most experts would agree that 20 mcg oral contraceptive pills should reduce the risks related to estrogen compared to pills containing 30-35mcg estrogen, more data are needed to support this theory. Note that breast tenderness may also be attributed to the progestin component.

Consider a pill from a different class of progestin (See box on page 30).

All low-dose OCs will improve acne and hirsutism. Ortho Tricyclen is the first OCP to gain FDA approval for this specific indication. If, after three cycles of OCP use, the patient's symptoms do not improve, try a different class of progestin.

Consider Depo-Provera.

The first 3 months are the most likely time for annoying problems, such as nausea and breakthrough bleeding and spotting to occur. If problems persist after the first 3 months and the woman is dissatisfied, offer another formulation.

There are many pill formulations available, and a variety of strategies to use based on the different components—primarily, the progestin component—to address problems. It should be noted, however, that all women metabolize synthetic hormones differently. While it makes sense to switch to certain formulations for certain problems as outlined below, occasionally a problem may be resolved just by switching to any other formulation.

Possible Side Effects of OCs
Common side effects of hormonal contraceptives can be categorized as relatively minor effects of estrogen or progestin. For contraceptive purposes, estrogen maintains the endometrium and progestins inhibit ovulation.

Progestins Used in Oral Contraceptives

The progestins used in oral contraceptives can be divided into two classes: Gonanes and Estranes

Gonanes (Levonorgestrel family)	Estranes (Norethindrone family)
levonorgestrel	norethindrone
desogestrel	norethindrone acetate
norgestimate	norethynodrel
gestodene*	ethynodiol diacetate
	lynestrenol*

One strategy for managing side effect-problems related to the progestin content of oral contraceptives is to switch to a different class of progestin. For example, switching from a norethindrone-containing OC to a levonorgestrel-containing OC may be effective for the management of breakthrough bleeding.

not available in OCs marketed in the United States

Side effects of estrogens include

- nausea
- breast tenderness
- vascular headaches
- irregular bleeding (especially with high doses)
- weight gain (bloating).

Side effects of progestins include

- spotting/breakthrough bleeding
- acne
- hirsutism
- weight gain
- oily skin, sebaceous cysts
- breast tenderness.

Management of the Side Effects of Combination Oral Contraceptives

Most of the side effects associated with the use of combination oral contraceptives (COCs) can be managed through a change in drug formulation or other simple measures.

Amenorrhea

Amenorrhea or bleeding that may be reduced to a negligible brown discharge is common on low-dose COCs, especially with time. COCs decrease the cyclical thickening of the endometrial lining. Subsequently, there is less to shed at the time of "menses." The best therapy for pill-induced amenorrhea is counseling before the patient starts the pill. The counseling is important because amenorrhea creates significant anxiety for some women and has been correlated with discontinuing use of the pill.

To manage:

1. *Assess the pregnancy risk and rule out an ectopic pregnancy:*

   - Has there been consistent use of the pill?

- Was there a late start of a new pill pack or an extension of the pill-free interval?
- Was there regular bleeding while on COCs prior to the onset of amenorrhea?
- Has the woman used rifampin, or griseofulvin, or other drugs that may

Need for Flexibility

Historically, the instructions women have been given about oral contraceptives have been fairly rigid. Women have been told to take 21 pills of active ingredients followed by 7 days of placebo pills or 7 pill-free days. Intended to mimic the natural 28-day cycle, this regimen has, however, been demonstrated to have potential problems. Ultrasound studies have shown that more than 10% of women have enlarged follicles before they start taking their next active pills. It is challenging for women to remember to take pills on a daily basis. If the goal is to increase correct and consistent birth control pill use to prevent unintended pregnancy, it may be wise to consider different options in pill administration to reduce risk of pregnancy and maximize noncontraceptive benefits.

First-Day Start Every Cycle
To reduce the risk of inadvertent ovulation and thus the risk of pregnancy, it has been suggested that the number of placebo pill days or pill-free days be reduced. One straightforward approach is to make every cycle a first day start. With this approach, women start the first pill of a pack on the first day of menses, and no backup protection is necessary. A woman who starts her pill pack on day one of menses and takes 21 active pills will typically begin withdrawal bleeding 2-3 days later. As soon as her next menses begins, she should discard the old pack (which may have several placebo pills remaining) and start her next pack of active pills. If a woman does not have any bleeding in 5 days after stopping the active pills, she should start the next pack anyway, unless she has signs or symptoms of pregnancy. The first day start is particularly useful for women who have a history of previous pill failure, who have breakthrough bleeding on the low-dose pills, and those who have menstrual migraine headaches. One disadvantage to this approach is that the day of the week the first pill is taken will change from

decrease the efficacy of the oral contraceptive?

■ Are there signs/symptoms of pregnancy, spotting or bleeding, or pelvic pain?

■ Perform beta HCC or other pregnancy test, if indicated.

in Prescribing OCs

month to month, a fact that has been found particularly confusing to young users.

Bi-Cycling or Tri-Cycling Pills

For years, clinicians have been able to manipulate a woman's menses to have it occur at a less inconvenient time—say, not on a honeymoon. The fact is that it is not absolutely necessary for a women to have withdrawal bleeding every month. Under progesterone influence, there is minimal buildup of the endometrium. Now, some women have experienced DMPA-induced amenorrhea—and they like it. The same goal can be achieved with monophasic pills given continuously without pill-free intervals. The first cycle a woman may start to experience breakthrough bleeding after 5- 6 weeks of pill use. At that point, she should stop taking the pills for 3-5 days, after which she should resume pill-taking. Usually the active pills will sustain amenorrhea for progressively longer periods of time. This amenorrhea may be helpful for women with dysmenorrhea, menstrual migraine headaches, or anemia due to menorrhagia or sickle-cell disease, as well as for women taking anticoagulation medication and those who have bleeding dyscrasias.

Summary

Once women are experienced with the pill and understand how it works, they may want to discuss with their healthcare provider the use of the pill to control their periods. Flexibility in the timing of menses may add considerably to the attractiveness of the pill. However, it must be remembered that if a woman does not use the pill correctly and consistently, there is no guarantee that she will not become pregnant. The added benefit of other payoffs such as control of periods may provide the woman with immediate positive feedback and result in her being more willing to invest in the effort to remember to take the pills.

2. *Treat in several ways:*

  ■ Do nothing. Amenorrhea is not harmful, and some women may appreciate the lack of periods. Explain that amenorrhea is not unhealthy. There is no buildup of uterine tissue.

  ■ To alleviate a patient's concerns about a possible pregnancy, consider use of body temperature on day 6 or 7 of inactive pill interval. If the temperature is less than 98°F, the patient is not pregnant.

  ■ If the patient desires more regular bleeding, switch to a different progestin.

Breakthrough Bleeding (BTB) or Spotting

With the low-dose COCs currently used, the majority of side effects are minimized. The most common side effect with COCs is intermenstrual spotting, which is primarily due to the very low estrogenic effect of the low-dose COCs. The low estrogenic impact on the endometrium, coupled with the progestin effect of endometrial atrophy, can result in spotting from the thinned endometrial lining.

To manage:

1. *Since the most common cause of BTB is incorrect use of the pill:*

  ■ Review pill-taking habits. COCs should ideally be taken within a 4-hour period every 24 hours (Progestin-only pills should be taken within a 3-hour window every 24 hours.)

  ■ Discuss the availability of other contraceptive methods, particularly DMPA or IUDs with women who have difficulty with daily pill-taking. Failure to start a new pack of pills by 2 days can result in ovulation in 30% of women.

  ■ For situations in which pills have been

skipped, offer emergency contraception.

■ Provide more than 1 month's pill supply, if possible, or provide a pack for "emergencies," such as "forgot to refill." This same pack can be used for emergency contraception as needed if it contains norgestrel or levonorgestrel.

2. *Consider other causes of bleeding, such as chlamydia, cervicitis, endometritis, and genital abrasions, ulcers or warts. Note that smoking increases the risk of breakthrough bleeding.*

3. *Increase estrogen dose and/or use a pill with a progestin with a longer half-life. A few head-to-head trials have shown slightly less BTB with these progestins, but the benefit may decrease over time. Avoid frequent switching of pills. Offer reassurance.*

■ Increase the pill dosage from 20mcg to 30mcg or 35mcg, as indicated.

■ Try a pill containing a different class of progestin. (See Table on page 30).

4. *Ask patients about use of medications, such as rifampin, griseofulvin, or dilantin, which can increase hormone clearance and result in breakthrough bleeding. Also ask about smoking, which increases risk of BTB.*

■ Advise patients taking these medications to use other forms of birth control—e.g., DMPA (Depo-Provera), barrier methods, or abstinence.

■ Consider use of a 50mcg COC. Use of these medications may be one of the only reasons to switch to that higher dose.

5. *Recognize psychosocial/sexual issues that may be involved in BTB. Pill-related bleeding can be*

problematic sexually for some women. In some religions, women who are bleeding must abstain from sex; this is particularly true in Orthodox Jewish traditions and among Muslim women. Vaginal bleeding can also be a barrier to oral sex for women. Always ask women considering using a contraceptive that may cause spotting/bleeding irregularity if she thinks this may cause problems with her sexual relationships.

Acne, Hirsutism, and Other Dermatologic Conditions

Generally there are few effects on the skin with low-dose COCs. All COCs will usually relieve acne and oily skin. Tricyclen has been approved by the FDA for the specific indication of acne. Approval for this indication is currently being sought for several other brands.

Occasionally, acne will develop when COCs are initiated. This can be resolved by switching to a different pill formulation. These same principles apply to women with excessive hair (hirsutism) or loss of hair.

Occasionally chloasma may develop as a result of estrogenic stimulation of melanocytes. This can result in darkened pigmentation on the face, as is common in pregnancy. Chloasma is rare with the use of low-dose COCs.

To manage:

1. *Switch to the lowest dose estrogen COC.*

2. *Consider contraceptives without estrogen.*

3. *Advise use of sunscreens.*

Chloasma usually resolves slowly after discontinuation of COCs; however, occasionally it may not resolve.

Breast Tenderness

Breast tenderness and fullness is most frequently related to the estrogen in COCs and occurs less often in sub-50mcg dose COCs.

To manage:

1. *Rule out other causes of breast tenderness, such as pregnancy or breast disease.*

2. *Switch to a COC with a lower dose of estrogen.*

3. *Try a different class of progestin.*

4. *Advise good bra support.*

The following are suggested by many clinicians— decreasing intake of methylxanthines (coffee, tea, chocolate, soft drinks) and use of vitamin E (4000 I.U. b.i.d.). These suggestions, while not supported by scientific data, are not harmful.

Nausea

Nausea is most common during the first few months of COC use; during use of the first pills in a pack; or when taking more than one pill because of a missed pill.

To manage:

1. *Inform patients that nausea decreases over time and when pills are taken on time.*

2. *Advise taking COCs with the evening meal or at bedtime.*

3. *Tell patients that if vomiting occurs within 2 hours of taking the pill, to take another pill.*

4. *Consider switching to a pill with less estrogen.*

Diminished Libido

All hormonal methods of contraception can decrease free testosterone. This may result in diminished libido in some patients. However, in other patients less worry about unintended pregnancy may result in increased libido.

To manage:

1. *Switch to a pill with a different class of progestin than the one the patient is currently using.*

2. *Explore other possible causes of decreased libido—for example, fear of STD/HIV, an unstable relationship, or other fears.*

3. *If diminished libido still persists, consider advising patient about an IUD or barrier contraceptives.*

Headaches

There is no evidence that COCs increase the incidence of tension headaches. There is considerable debate as to whether COCs impact vascular headaches. In general, women who have migraines with focal neurologic symptoms are advised not to use hormonal contraceptives with estrogens. Focal neurological symptoms include episodes of extremity paresthesias, blindness, or seizures. However, women who have no focal neurological signs may use low-dose COCs with follow-up to assess any changes in headache patterns, such as increases in headache frequency or severity or the development of neurologic symptoms. It is important to remember that severe headaches and neurologic symptoms may signal an impending stroke.

To manage:

1. *Initial evaluation—Any headache in a COC user that is increasing in frequency or severity or is accompanied by neurologic symptoms should be evaluated carefully. Central nervous system tumors should be included in the differential diagnosis. Do not assume that new-onset significant headaches are related to use of COCs.*

   ■ Obtain a detailed history that includes family history of migraines or diagnosis of migraine, sinusitis, allergies, temporomandibular joint (TMJ) syndrome, dental disease, or infections (meningitis), galactorrhea (pituitary adenoma), or history of brain tumors.

- Remember **OLDCART**. Ask about the

  Onset of the pain;

  Location of the pain;

  Duration of the pain;

  Character of the pain;

  Aggravating and/or **A**lleviating factors that affect the pain;

  Radiation of the pain; and

  Treatments/therapies tried.

- Always ask about use of prescription drugs; substance abuse, especially cocaine (crack) amphetamines, alcohol; use of over-the-counter (OTC) drugs, especially Sudafed® and herbs (ephedra); intake of alcohol, nicotine, and caffeine; and use of vitamins.

- Ask about neurologic symptoms that may accompany the headache—symptoms such as nausea or vomiting, dizziness, blurred vision, loss of vision, scotomata, syncope, loss of speech, weakness, numbness, tingling, or behavior changes.

2. *Physical assessment of COC patient with severe headache:*

- Measure blood pressure.
- Perform fundoscopic examination to evaluate signs of papilledema, suggestive of intracranial pressure.
- Evaluate cranial nerves and deep tendon reflexes (DTRs). Perform neurological exam.
- Palpate temporal area for a tender temporal

The Steroid Content of Some Currently Available Oral Contraceptives

Trademark	Manufacturer	Estrogen	Estrogen mcg per tab	Progestogen	Progestogen mg per tab
50 MICROGRAMS ESTROGEN					
Ovral*	Wyeth-Ayerst	Ethinyl Estradiol	50	Norgestrel	0.5
Norlestrin® 2.5/50	Parke-Davis	Ethinyl Estradiol	50	Norethindrone Acetate	2.5
Norlestrin® 1/50	Parke-Davis	Ethinyl Estradiol	50	Norethindrone Acetate	1.0
Demulen® 1/50	Searle	Ethinyl Estradiol	50	Ethynodiol Diacetate	1.0
Norinyl® 1+50	Searle	Mestranol	50	Norethindrone	1.0
Ortho-Novum® 1/50	Ortho	Mestranol	50	Norethindrone	1.0
Ovcon® 50	Bristol-Myers Squibb	Ethinyl Estradiol	50	Norethindrone	1.0
PROGESTIN-ONLY OCS					
Ovrette®	Wyeth-Ayerst			Norgestrel	0.075
Micronor®	Ortho			Norethindrone	0.35
Nor-QD®	Searle			Norethindrone	0.35
SUB 50 MICROGRAMS ESTROGEN					
Alesse™	Wyeth-Ayerst	Ethinyl Estradiol	20	Levonorgestrel	0.1
Lo/Ovral®	Wyeth-Ayerst	Ethinyl Estradiol	30	Norgestrel	0.3
Nordette®	Wyeth-Ayerst	Ethinyl Estradiol	30	Levonorgestrel	0.15
Levlen®	Berlex	Ethinyl Estradiol	30	Levonorgestrel	0.15
Ortho-Novum® 1/35	Ortho	Ethinyl Estradiol	35	Norethindrone	1.0
Ortho-Novum® 10/11	Ortho	Ethinyl Estradiol	35	Norethindrone	0.5 (10d)
					1.0 (11d)
Modicon®	Ortho	Ethinyl Estradiol	35	Norethindrone	0.5
Ortho-Cyclen®	Ortho	Ethinyl Estradiol	35	Norgestimate	0.25
Ortho-Cept®	Ortho	Ethinyl Estradiol	30	Desogestrel	0.15
Desogen®	Organon	Ethinyl Estradiol	30	Desogestrel	0.15

Product	Manufacturer	Estrogen	mcg	Progestin	mg	
Jenest®	Organon	Ethinyl Estradiol	35	Norethindrone	0.5	(7d)
					1.0	(14d)
Loestrin® 1/20	Parke-Davis	Ethinyl Estradiol	20	Norethindrone Acetate	1.0	
Loestrin® 1.5/30	Parke-Davis	Ethinyl Estradiol	30	Norethindrone Acetate	1.5	
Demulen® 1/35	Searle	Ethinyl Estradiol	35	Ethynodiol Diacetate	1.0	
Norinyl® 1+35	Searle	Ethinyl Estradiol	35	Norethindrone	1.0	
Brevicon®	Searle	Ethinyl Estradiol	35	Norethindrone	0.5	
Ovcon® 35	Bristol-Myers Squibb	Ethinyl Estradiol	35	Norethindrone	0.4	
TRIPHASICS						
Triphasil	Wyeth-Ayerst	Ethinyl Estradiol	30	Levonorgestrel	0.05	(6d)
			40		0.075	(5d)
			30		0.125	(10d)
Tri-Levlen®	Berlex	Ethinyl Estradiol	30	Levonorgestrel	0.05	(6d)
			40		0.075	(5d)
			30		0.125	(10d)
Ortho-Novum® 7/7/7	Ortho	Ethinyl Estradiol	35	Norethindrone	0.5	(7d)
			35		0.75	(7d)
			35		1.0	(7d)
Ortho Tri-Cyclen®	Ortho	Ethinyl Estradiol	35	Norgestimate	0.18	(7d)
			35		0.215	(7d)
			35		0.25	(7d)
Tri-Norinyl	Searle	Ethinyl Estradiol	35	Norethindrone	0.5	(7d)
			35		1.0	(9d)
			35		0.5	(5d)
Estrostep®	Parke-Davis	Ethinyl Estradiol	20	Norethindrone Acetate	1.0	(5d)
			30		1.0	(7d)
			35		1.0	(9d)

Trademarks and registered trademarks are as of Feb. 1996.   *Does not include all OCs.

artery, suggestive of temporal arteritis. Temporal arteritis is an emergency and the patient must be referred to a neurologist or ophthalmologist immediately to avoid risk of permanent blindness.

- Palpate frontal and maxillary sinus areas for tenderness to rule out sinusitis.

3. *Treatment Plan*

- If the COC user has abnormal fundoscopy, cranial nerve assessment, or DTRs or has neurologic symptoms, refer patient for a CAT scan or MRI and discontinue COCs.
- If patient has headaches related to TMJ syndrome or sinusitis, treat those disorders or refer for treatment and continue on COC's.
- If patient does not have neurologic symptoms or findings and the headaches are not increasing in frequency or severity, then provide one or two cycles of COCs and have patient report any danger signs/symptoms to you immediately.
- Tension headaches can be treated with aspirin, nonsteroidal antiinflammatory agents (NSAIDs), stress reduction, massage, or relaxation techniques.

Note: Patients with menstrual migraines may find relief with COC use. Patients who find that they have menstrual migraine during the pill-free interval may shorten or delete the pill-free interval.

Health Benefits of Combination Oral Contraceptives

Several studies have shown that the use of combination oral contraceptives is associated with certain noncontraceptive health benefits—for example, a reduction in risk of endometrial and

Health Benefits of
Combination Oral Contraceptives*

*Use of COCs reduce the risk of
endometrial and ovarian cancers*

Years of COC Use	Reduction in Endometrial Cancer	Reduction in Ovarian Cancer
4 Years	54%	40%
8 Years	66%	53%
12 Years	72%	60%

*Although these benefits are based on 50mcg pills, the benefits are thought to be caused by cessation of ovulation. Therefore, these benefits should apply to all COCs regardless of the estrogen dose and probably also apply to progestin-only methods.

ovarian cancers, even in women who have mutations in BRCA1 or BRCA2 gene that put them at high lifetime risk of ovarian cancer.

There are also studies reporting that use of combination oral contraceptives reduces the incidence of ectopic pregnancies. The ectopic rate in non-contracepting women is 26:10,000 women. For women with tubal ligation, the ectopic rate is 3.2:10,000 women, and for women using COCs the ectopic rate is 0.05:10,000 women.

COC use is also associated with a decrease in breast disease, pelvic inflammatory disease (PID), anemia, ovarian cysts, premenstrual syndrome (PMS), and dysmenorrhea.

Bone mineralization has also been shown to increase with COC use, up to 12% with over 10 years of COC use in premenopausal users.

Managing the Side Effects of
Hormonal Implants and Injectables

The most common side effect associated with The Norplant System® implant and with the injectable

Depo-Provera is spotting/irregular bleeding. Depo-Provera has also been associated with amenorrhea and possibly with changes in bone density.

Careful counseling of patients before insertion of The Norplant System® or initiation of Depo-Provera injections results in better acceptance of menstrual irregularities, if they do occur. Women become most concerned about side effects when they have not been adequately informed about them. When women are prepared for side effects, they tend to take them in stride. A counseling session of 45 minutes is not unreasonable and may be done in groups.

It is also important for the clinician to remember that uterine bleeding may be a sign of ectopic pregnancy, endometritis, cancer, or coagulopathies, especially Von Willebrand's disease.

Spotting/Irregular Bleeding
Both The Norplant System® and DMPA are associated with irregular bleeding, and Depo-Provera with amenorrhea.

To manage:

1. *Consider observation and counsel the patient not to be concerned about her blood count. It is probably higher than when she started use of the method.*

2. *Provide two or three cycles of low-dose COCs to patients starting DMPA or The Norplant System®. Usually patients' cycles become more regular over time. Giving concomitant COCs can regulate the menses for the first few months when the cycle is usually the most disrupted.*

3. *For The Norplant System® users, consider use of prostaglandin inhibitors, in the form of NSAIDS, which can reduce bleeding in 75% of patients. If the patient begins to have prolonged bleeding episodes, advise ibuprofen, 400mg t.i.d.*

for 3-5 days; 75% of patients will then stop bleeding. The dose can be titrated downward in subsequent cycles. However, patients with asthma or gastrointestinal disorders, especially ulcer disease, should avoid NSAIDs.

4. For Depo-Provera users, give estrogens: oral 17-beta estradiol (Estrace) 2mg daily for 7-10 days; oral conjugated estrogen (Premarin), 1.25mcg daily for 7-10 days; or 0.1mg transdermal patch. This should probably be avoided in Norplant System® users who may be ovulating. The contraceptive mechanism in some Norplant System® users involves the effect of progestin on sperm entry. Estrogen could reverse this effect.

Changes in Bone Density
Studies on the possible effects of DMPA on bone density, particularly in adolescents are ongoing. The effect of DMPA on bone density is thought to be similar to that in lactating women—that is, that decreases in bone density are reversible once the drug therapy or lactation is discontinued.

To manage:

1. Advise women using DMPA to maintain good nutrition and especially to eat foods rich in calcium.

2. Consider advising calcium supplementation of 1000-15000mg/day for adolescents and 1000mg/day for adult women.

Possible Non-Contraceptive Benefits Associated with DMPA Use
DMPA is an excellent contraceptive for women with certain chronic disorders. For example, for women who have a seizure disorder, use of DMPA has been shown in some studies to reduce the frequency and

severity of seizures. And, for women with sickle-cell disease, the drug reduces the severity and frequency of sickle-cell crises.

DMPA can be taken by women taking anti-tuberculosis medications and anti-seizure medications.

Emergency Contraception

Emergency contraception is a way to reduce the risk of pregnancy after sex. It is sometimes known as the "morning after" treatment, or "post-coital" contraception. The term "emergency contraception" is preferred because the methods are best suited for limited "emergency" use and can be used for several days after unprotected intercourse, not just the morning after.

Marketing of an emergency contraceptive packet was approved by the FDA in 1998. This was an important step to reduce the unacceptably high number of unintended pregnancies (3.2 million each year) in the United States and the need for abortion.

Methods—There are three methods currently used for emergency contraception.

- FDA-Approved Emergency Contraceptive Pills (ECPs)—In 1998 the FDA approved the marketing of a four-pill emergency contraceptive packet called Preven®. The pills each contain 500mg levonorgestrel and 50mcg estradiol. Two are taken within 72 hours of unprotected sex and two more are taken 12 hours later. The major side effect reported is nausea and vomiting.

  The use of regular oral contraceptive pills in higher-than-usual doses for emergency contraception, known as the Yuzpe regimen, was deemed "safe and effective" for use as "after the fact" birth control by the FDA in

Some Contraceptive Pills That Can Be Used For Emergency Contraception

Yuzpe Method

Ovral — 500mcg norgestrel/50mcg ethinyl estradiol
    2 active pills taken within 72 hours of unprotected sex,
    followed by 2 pills 12 hours later

Lo/Ovral — 300mcg norgestrel/30mcg ethinyl estradiol

or

Nordette/Levlen — 150mcg 1-norgestrel/30mcg ethinyl estradiol
    4 active pills taken within 72 hours of unprotected sex
    followed by 4 pills 12 hours later

Progestin-Only Method

Ovrette — 75mcg norgestrel (progestin-only mini-pill)
    20 active pills taken within 72 hours of unprotected sex
    followed by 20 pills 12 hours later

March 1997. This amounted to a strong endorsement of "off-label" use of seven brands of regular oral contraceptives for emergency contraception. However, the 1998 decision marked the first time that the FDA approved the marketing of a packet designed specifically for emergency contraception use.

- Progestin-only pills can also be used for emergency contraception. Treatment must be initiated within 48 hours after unprotected intercourse. Recent data suggest progestin-only pills are equally effective as, but cause fewer side effects than, the Yuzpe method.

- Insertion of a Copper T IUD (Paragard-T®) within 5 days after unprotected intercourse also can prevent pregnancy. However, insertion is contraindicated if a cervical STD cannot be ruled out.

When Needed—No contraceptive method is fail-safe, and few couples can use their method perfectly every time they have intercourse. Emergency contraception provides an important safety net when:

- a condom breaks;
- no contraception is used;
- a woman misses 2 or more birth control pills or starts a pack 2 or more days late;
- a woman misses the deadline for a contraceptive injection;
- a diaphragm slips out of place;
- sex occurs unexpectedly and without protection;
- a woman is raped.

How Do ECPs Work?—The mechanism of action of ECPs has not been clearly established. Several studies have shown that ECPs can inhibit or delay ovulation. It has also been suggested that ECPs may prevent implantation by altering the endometrium. However, whether the endometrial changes observed in some studies would be sufficient to prevent implantation is not known. ECPs also may prevent fertilization or transport of sperm or ova, but no data exist regarding these possible mechanisms. ECPs do not interrupt an established pregnancy.

How Effective Are ECPs?—Use of Preven® or the Yuzpe method reduces the risk of pregnancy by about 75%. Typically, if 100 women have unprotected sex once during the second or third week of their cycle, 8 would become pregnant. With ECPs, only 2 would become pregnant.

Are ECPs Safe?—No serious or long-term complications have been definitively linked to use of the Yuzpe regimen (Preven®) in Europe, where ECPs are widely used. Published studies report no evidence-based contraindications to use of the method.

It should be noted that the patient using emergency contraception may be at risk for a STD from the unprotected sex.

If The Pills Fail, Are There Risks to The Fetus?— While no studies have assessed the teratogenic effects associated specifically with ECPs, there are no biomedical reasons to expect an increased risk of birth defects if ECPs fail. There is no evidence that combined oral contraceptive use, even of high-dose pills (150 mcg per day ethinyl estradiol), has any teratogenic effects.

Is Repeated Use of ECPs Harmful?—Repeated use of ECPs poses no known health risks to women. Of greatest concern is the increased likelihood of pregnancy with repeated use. For this reason, women using ECPs should be advised to begin using a regular contraceptive after ECP treatment.

For More Information

Call the Emergency Contraception Hotline at
1-888-NOT-2-LATE

Visit the Emergency Contraception Web Site at
http://opr.princeton.edu/ec/

Information concerning emergency contraception was excepted from "Facts About Emergency Contraception," produced by PATH.

This chapter was prepared by Susan Wysocki, RNC, BSN, NP; Sharon Myoji Schnare, RN, FNP, CNM, MSN; and Anita Nelson, MD, with the editorial assistance of Barbara Tchabovsky.

Notes

CHAPTER 3

SEXUALLY TRANSMITTED AND OTHER INFECTIOUS DISEASES OF THE FEMALE GENITAL TRACT

Sexually transmitted diseases (STDs) are infections transmitted from one person to another, usually by sexual contact. These infections can be spread from skin to skin contact; by sharing secretions from the penis, vagina, mouth, or rectum; and through contact with blood. STDs can be spread from man to woman, woman to man, woman to woman, and man to man. STDs can cause pain, infertility, scarring of the skin, and even death. Some, such as human papillomavirus-venereal warts, are associated with the development of cervical cancer in women and may be associated with the development of genital cancers in men.

Common curable STDs affecting women include syphilis, gonorrhea, chlamydia trachomatis, and trichomoniasis. STDs that have no definitive cure, but can be treated palliatively, include acquired immunodeficiency syndrome (AIDS); herpes simplex; human papillomavirus (HPV), or venereal warts; and hepatitis B. AIDS can be transmitted by sexual contact and through blood (e.g., through sharing of needles) and from a pregnant woman to her child during pregnancy, childbirth, or breast-feeding.

Other infections of the female genital tract, such as bacterial vaginosis and candidiasis, are not usually sexually transmitted, often resulting from a change in the ecosystem of the vagina, but they can be sexually transmitted. Finally, this chapter will include a brief discussion of another common female disorder—urinary tract infections.

Prevalence and Identification of <u>Those At High Risk</u>

Vaginitis and sexually transmitted diseases are very common, with more than half—perhaps 75%—of all women experiencing at least one type of infection during their lifetimes. Women at risk for STDs come from every socioeconomic group, culture, age group, and workplace.

Although healthcare providers should counsel all patients about the risks of sexually transmitted diseases, it is also important to identify those at high risk. Among those considered at high risk of acquiring an STD are prostitutes, people with multiple sex partners, intravenous drug users, and people under the age of 20. It is important that patients be told that an STD may not have any obvious symptoms. The following questions may help a healthcare provider identify a patient at high risk of acquiring an STD. Ask:

- *How many partners have you had in your lifetime? over the last year?*

- *Is your sex partner having sex with more than one person?*

If the answer to either or both of these questions indicates a non-mutually monogamous relationship, then ask if a condom is used with every sexual act. If it is not, the patient definitely needs counseling about STDs and symptoms to watch for.

Clinicians should also be alert to other specific conditions or factors that may make a woman more likely to develop a nonsexually transmitted type of vaginitis and/or a sexually transmitted disease. Awareness of lifestyle changes also alerts the clinician to the need for counseling. Ask, for example:

- *Have you being taking antibiotics recently?*

- *Do you douche regularly?*

- *Have you recently had a new sex partner?*

- *Do you have diabetes?*

- *Have you changed toilet paper, soaps, detergents, or personal products, or have you been bathing in chlorinated pools or taking bubble baths?*

- *Have you recently had rough and/or lengthy sexual intercourse?*

- *Have you begun or changed the use of any drugs?*

- *What do you do to protect yourself from STDs?*

General Signs and Symptoms in Assessing the Possibility of Infection

The primary care provider is often the first provider that a woman who is experiencing genital-related symptoms, even mild ones, approaches. It is very important that the primary care provider be alert to all the symptoms that may signal a sexually transmitted or otherwise acquired infection affecting the female genitourinary tract. And, since many infections may be asymptomatic, even for prolonged periods of time, it is important that the routine evaluation of a female patient not only elicit information concerning possible symptoms—symptoms the patient may be overlooking—but also actively seek to identify any signs of infection. As stated earlier, questions concerning recent lifestyle changes can elicit valuable information and alert the provider and patient to possible increased risks.

Among the physical signs/symptoms/topics that the provider should be vigilant about are the presence of

- *pain or discomfort*

- *a discharge and its odor*
- *unusual bleeding*
- *dysuria*
- *frequency*
- *fever - unexplained*
- *lesions*
- *itching*
- *enlarged lymph nodes*
- *dyspareunia*
- *abdominal pain*

Common Infectious Diseases

There are several infectious diseases that are almost exclusively sexually transmitted, some that may or may not be, and some that usually are not. The following pages provide a brief overview of major infectious genital/urinary diseases, outlining symptoms, diagnosis, treatment, follow-up, and prevention, where applicable. The discussions are not exhaustive, but rather highlight the signs/symptoms commonly observed and treatment options widely used.

Consult the latest recommendations of the Centers for Disease Control (CDC) concerning treatment options, dosages, and use during pregnancy.

Bacterial Vaginosis (BV)
Gardnerella vaginalis vaginitis (GVV) and other bacterial species

The most prevalent form of vaginitis among women of childbearing age

Not usually considered a sexually transmitted disease, but may be considered sexually associated since semen may help alter the normal vaginal environment

Treatment of male partner not found helpful

Risk Factors:
  use of antibiotics
  douching
  sexual intercourse
  (Diet changes and stress may also play a role,
  although there is no scientific data to support this.)

Signs & Symptoms may include:
  malodorous thin grey/white discharge
  itching and external erythema–sometimes
  fishy odor, especially after intercourse

Diagnosis:
  observation of thin, dull, greyish, malodorous,
    homogenous adherent discharge
  wet mount showing bacterial clue cells adhering
    to cell wall
  positive "Whiff test" – fishy odor when KOH added to
    vaginal secretion
  pH > 4.7

Treatment Options:
  Metronidazole (Flagyl) 500mg PO twice for 7 days
  Clindamycin cream 2% inserted vaginally for 7 days
    (safe during first trimester of pregnancy)
  Metronidazole gel, 0.75 vaginally b.i.d. for 5 days
  Metronidazole, 2g PO as a single dose
  Clindamycin 300mg PO b.i.d. for 7 days
  (During the second and third trimester of
    pregnancy, oral metronidazole, 250mg t.i.d,
    for 7 days is preferred)

Follow-Up:
  Since the disease is associated with preterm and
  low-birth-weight infants, pregnant women and
  those considering becoming pregnant should be
  counseled accordingly.

Candidiasis
Candida albicans, Candida glabrata, Candida tropicalis

Other names: monilia, yeast infection, vulvovaginal candidiasis (VVC)

Found in about 25% of women with healthy vaginal environments

A recurrent and irritating form of vaginitis that is not usually sexually transmitted, but can be

Predisposing Factors:
    antibiotic use
    obesity
    diabetes
    HIV infection or other immunosuppressive
        disorder
    pregnancy

Signs & Symptoms may include:
    itching
    dysuria
    erythema
    cottage cheese (white and thick) discharge

Diagnosis:
    wet mount (KOH preparation) showing yeast
    pH <4.5

Treatment Options:
    Terconazole (Terazol) cream or suppositories
    A variety of topical agents are available over-the-
        counter, including Miconazole (Monistat) cream
        or suppositories
    Fluconazole (Diflucan) 150mg PO once (not
        recommended during pregnancy)

Follow-Up:
    Intercourse should be avoided during course of
        treatment.
    Cream and suppositories may decrease integrity of
        latex condoms and diaphragms.

Persistent infections may indicate underlying disease such as diabetes, HIV, or other immunosuppressive disorder.

Prevention:
Consider use of an antifungal agent when taking any systemic antibiotic.

Avoid a warm, moist genital environment. Be sure to dry the genital area before dressing, and wear cotton underwear.

Although *Lactobacillus acidophilus* yogurt has been recommended by many clinicians for use as a dietary supplement or intravaginally there is no evidence that it is helpful. The *Lactobacillus* in yogurt is not the same type as *Lactobacillus* in the normal vagina.

A reduction in stress and diet improvements have not been scientifically validated, but are not harmful.

Chlamydia
Chlamydia trachomatis

The most commonly reported STD in the United States

A leading cause of infertility, ectopic pregnancy, and pelvic inflammatory disease (PID)

Transmitted through sexual contact or during childbirth

Incubation:
3-30 days

Signs & Symptoms may include:
mucopurulent cervical or vaginal discharge
friable cervix
adnexal tenderness

Note:
Use of topical vaginal creams and ointments may weaken latex in condoms and diaphragms.

---

uterine tenderness
enlarged femoral lymph nodes
dysuria
unusual bleeding
partner with discharge/dysuria
either partner may be asymptomatic

Diagnosis:

wet mount of discharge may reveal numerous
WBCs

antigen detection tests - e.g., Chlamydiazyme or
Microtrak - if available

culture ("gold standard") is expensive, requires
special storage, and takes several days for results

presumptive diagnosis: muculopurulent cervical
discharge

Treatment Options:

Doxycline, 100mg PO b.i.d. for 7-10 days
(not during pregnancy)

Azithromycin, 1 gm PO once

Ofloxacin, 300 mg PO b.i.d. for 7 days (but not
in patients under 17 or in patients who are
pregnant)

Erythromycin, 500mg PO q.i.d. for 7 days (safe
during pregnancy)

Amoxocillin, 500mg PO t.i.d. for 7 days (safe
during pregnancy)

Follow-Up:

Arrange for treatment of partners, and consider
testing for other STDS since there is a high rate
of concurrent disease.

Gonorrhea

Neisseria gonorrhoeae

Transmission through sexual contact and childbirth

A leading cause of PID

Incubation:

1-14 days
average: 3-7 days

Signs & Symptoms may include:
mucopurulent cervical or vaginal discharge
friable cervix
adnexal tenderness
uterine tenderness
enlarged femoral lymph nodes
dysuria
unusual bleeding or not on pill
partner has discharge/dysuria
either partner may be asymptomatic

Diagnosis:
culture using Thayer-Martin medium

Treatment Options:
Ceftriaxone, 125mg (IM) in single dose
Cefixime, 400mg PO in single dose
Ciprofloxacin, 500mg PO in single dose (not during pregnancy)
Ofloxacin, 400mg PO in a single dose (not during pregnancy)
plus treatment for presumed chlamydia with
Doxycycline 100mg b.i.d. for 7 days (not during pregnancy) or
Azithromycin 1g PO (safe during pregnancy) or
Doxycycline 100mg b.i.d. for 7 days (not during pregnancy)

Follow-Up:
Arrange for treatment of partners.
Test of cure is indicated if compliance is questionable or if re-infection occurs. Then, retest 3 weeks after treatment.

Hepatitis B
Hepatitis B virus (HBV)

Transmission parenterally, sexually, or perinatally

Many cases never diagnosed because of nonspecific viral symptoms

May be mild, in a chronic state, or progress to serious liver disease

Incubation Period:
    1 -6 months
    average: 12 weeks

Risk Factors:
    intravenous drug use
    multiple sex partners
    being a partner of an HBV carrier
    being a health worker in contact with blood
    for an infant, an infected mother

Signs & Symptoms may include:
    jaundice
    fatigue
    clay-colored stools
    dark amber urine
    nausea, vomiting, diarrhea
    liver tenderness
    may be no apparent clinical symptoms

Diagnosis:
    sexual/drug history
    urinalysis
    blood test - hepatitis panel
    physical exam: generally negative but liver may be
        palpable

Treatment Options:
    no pharmacologic treatment available
    rest
    elevation of immune system
    elimination of toxins: alcohol, drugs
    increase in carbohydrate and protein intake
    a low-fat diet
    a high-potency multivitamin

Follow-Up:
    Advise on preventing transmission - e.g.,
        use of latex condoms.
    Advise on vaccination of partners and other
        close contacts.

Herpes
Herpes simplex virus (HSV)

HSV-2 possibly present in more than 30% of the U.S. population

Transmission primarily by direct contact (e.g. kissing, sexual contact, vaginal delivery) when the infected person is shedding the virus

Incubation Period:
2-10 days
clinical stage: 12-20 days

Signs & Symptoms may include:
vesicles and ulcers
swollen femoral lymph nodes
dysuria
severe vulvar pain
flu-like symptoms
may be no apparent symptoms

Diagnosis:
clinical presentation
herpes culture (expensive, with high false negative rate)
indirect immunoperoxidase
direct immunofluorescence

Treatment Options:
General measures: sitz baths; dry aloe vera gel; use of loose undergarments; prudent use of anesthetic gels (which have potential for systemic absorption and side effects if misused)

Initial:
Acyclovir 400mg, PO t.i.d. for 7 days
Acyclovir 200 mg capsules PO 5 times a day for 7 days
Famciclovir, 250mg PO 5 times a day for 7 days
Valacyclovir, 1g PO b.i.d. for 7 days

Recurrent and Suppressant:
Acyclovir, 400mg PO b.i.d.

Famciclovir, 125mg PO b.i.d.

Valacyclovir, 500mg PO once a day

Supressant therapy is indicated if patient has 6 recurrences within a year.

Follow-Up:

Discuss use of condoms and consider testing for HIV if serious infections are present or there are frequently recurrent episodes.

Prevention:

prophylactic administration of acyclovir if patient meets criteria (6 recurrences in 1 year)

rest

(Although not supported by scientific data, administration of folic acid [400mcg daily] and vitamin C [2000-3000mg daily]; elimination of toxins [e.g., alcohol]; and reduction of stress are not harmful and are thought to be useful by some clinicians.)

HIV: Human Immunodeficiency Virus

Transmission through sexual contact with infected body fluids; through contact with infected blood or blood products; or from an infected woman to her infant prenatally, at delivery, or through breastfeeding

Risk Factors:

anal sexual activity

multiple sexual partners

intravenous drug use

intercourse with prostitutes

previous STDs

blood transfusions before mid-1980s

Signs & Symptoms may include:

chronic yeast infections

fever

clinical signs of unresolving HPV infection

multiple infections

weight loss

skin lesions

fatigue

Diagnosis:
    history, including sexual history and drug use
      history
    HIV antibody blood tests (e.g., ELISA, Western blot)
    polymerase chain reaction (PCR) to determine
      viral load

Treatment:
    holistic regime with goal of elevating immune
      system
    treatment of opportunistic infections
    suppressive therapy (referral to a specialist for
      treatment regimens)

HPV - Human Papilloma Virus
Genital Warts *(Condylomata acuminata)*

More than 20 strains of the virus associated with
genital infections

Most common viral sexually transmitted disease

Usually, but not always, spread by sexual contact

Some strains of the virus associated with the
development of cervical dysplasia

Incubation:
    varies

Signs & Symptoms may include:
    pink to grey appearance
    dry, crusty flat or pedunculated lesions on vulva
      and cervix
    itching

Diagnosis:
    visual inspection of vulva, vagina, and cervix
    applying acetic acid 5% solution will cause HPV
      lesions to turn white
    Pap smear
    colposcopy
    biopsy
    use of serological test for syphilis to rule out
      condylomata lata

Treatment Options:
  Patient Applied:
    Imiquimod 5% cream 3 times a week at night, wash off after 6-10 hours; can be used for up to 16 weeks (not for use during pregnancy)
    Podofilox, 0.5% solution or gel to be applied twice a day for 3 days, followed by 4 days off treatment and then a repeat of cycle (not to be used during pregnancy)
  Provider Administered:
    Podophyllin 10%-25% - apply directly to lesion, wash off in 1-4 hours (not for use during pregnancy)
    Trichloroacetic acid (TCA), 85% - apply directly to lesions; allow to dry until a frosting develops. Repeat once a week as needed
    Cryotherapy – Liquid nitrogen or cryoprobe applied to lesion every 1-2 weeks.
    Laser removal of warts

Follow-Up:
  Women with history of HPV should have regular Pap smears. Self-examination of external genitals should also be recommended.

Prevention:
  use of condoms
  avoidance of multiple sex partners
  not smoking
  (Although not supported by scientific data, administration of folic acid [400mcg daily] and vitamin C [2000-3000mg daily]; elimination of toxins [e.g., alcohol]; and reduction of stress are not harmful and are thought to be useful by some clinicians.)

Molluscum contagiosum
Molluscum contagiosum virus (MCV) - A pox virus

Benign, viral infection that is usually self-limited, but may be difficult to eradicate in persons with HIV

Transmission primarily sexual in adults

Incubation:
　　1 week - 6 months
　　average: 2-3 months

Signs & Symptoms may include:
　　small, firm umbilicated lesions on vulva or trunk

Diagnosis:
　　visual inspection

Treatment:
　　observation or superficial incision and expression
　　　of contents
　　liquid nitrogen

Pediculosis pubis
Pubic lice or crabs

Highest incidence in young adults (15-25 years)

Signs & Symptoms may include:
　　intense itching, often leading to skin irritation
　　crab louse moving in pubic area and perianal area

Diagnosis:
　　observation of adult adult lice moving in pubic
　　　hair and of eggs (nits) as tiny white dots in hair

Treatment Options:
　　Lindane shampoo 1% - leave on for 4 minutes
　　　and then wash off
　　Permethrin 1% - apply for 10 minutes and then
　　　wash off

Follow-Up:
　　Contact partners to determine if they are
　　　infected.
　　Clothing and household items need to be disinfected
　　　by washing in hot water or treating with
　　　pyrethrin-containing products (Black Flag)

Syphilis
(Treponema pallidum)

A complex, sexually transmitted disease that can lead
to serious systemic disease and even death if untreated

Incubation Period:
10 - 90 days
average: 3 weeks

Signs & Symptoms may include:
Primary Stage: Painless ulcerated lesion on the
vagina or cervix (chancre) or elsewhere at site
of exposure
Secondary stage (2-6 weeks): maculopapular rash
on palms and/or soles, condylomata lata (fleshy,
moist tissue growths), lymphadenopathy, flulike
symptoms, alopecia
Latent Stage: tertiary syphilis involves the cardiovascular, central nervous, and muscular systems

Diagnosis/Laboratory:
serology: Venereal Disease Research Laboratory
(VDRL), Rapid Plasma Reagin (RPR), Fluorescent
Treponemal Antibody Absorbed (FTA,ABS),
Microhemagglutination Assay for Antibody to
Treponema pallidum (MHA-TP)

Treatment Options:
Early syphilis of <1 year-duration:
Benzathine penicillin G2.4 million units (IM) in a
single dose, or alternatively, if patient is allergic to
penicillin, Doxycycline 100 mg PO b.i.d. for 2 weeks
Early syphilis of >1 year duration:
Benzathine penicillin G2.4 million units (IM)
weekly for 3 weeks; or alternatively, Doxycycline
100 mg PO b.i.d. for 4 weeks.
Late Stage:
Penicillin G 7.2 million units in 3 doses, or
Doxycycline, 100 mg b.i.d. for 4 weeks
Consult latest CDC recommendations for treatment
options for penicillin-allergic pregnant women, for doxy-
cycliine-intolerant patients, for patients with congenital
syphilis, and for patients with both syphilis and HIV.

Follow-Up:
Stress importance of patients taking all

doses of medication. Advise patient of the possibility of Jarisch-Herxheimer reaction and tell patient to take nonsteroidal anti-inflammatory drugs (NSAIDs) if fever or chills occur.
Early syphilis: Reexamine in 1 week; Repeat serologies at 1,3,6, and 12 months after treatment. Repeat HIV test in 3 - 6 months.
Late syphilis: Repeat serology at 3, 6, 12, and 24 months after start of treatment.

Trichomoniasis
Trichomonas vaginalis

Sexual contact primary method of transmission

Incubation Period:
no finite period

Signs & Symptoms may include:
malodorous, copious, frothy, often yellow-green vaginal secretions
pelvic pain
dysuria
dyspareunia
erythesia
edema
pruritis

Diagnosis:
physical examination, sometimes showing vulvar erythema, edema, and/or occasionally, petechial lesions —"strawberry cervix"
mobile trichomonads in saline wet mount
vaginal culture or positive fluorescent antibody
Pap smear if verified by examination
pH >4.5

Treatment Options:
Metronidazole 2g PO in a single dose
Metronidazole 500mg PO b.i.d. for 7 days

Follow-Up:
Treat partners.

Advise patients to avoid alcohol during treatment
and for a day afterward.

Urinary Tract Infection (UTI) - Cystitis

Sometimes associated with sexual intercourse—
"honeymoon" cystitis

Symptoms:
frequency
dysuria
hematuria
itching
vulvar or abdominal pain
cramping
flank pain
nocturea incontinence

Diagnosis:
WBC and/or RBC on Dipstix of urine
urinalysis
urine culture and sensitivity.

Treatment Options:
Uncomplicated UTIs can be treated with 3-day
treatment which has been found to be just as
effective as traditional 7-10 day treatments.
TMP-SMX (Trimethoprim Sulfamethoxazole
PO b.i.d. for 3 days
Nitrofurantoin (Macrodantin), 100mg PO b.i.d. for
3 days
force fluids

*This chapter was prepared by Susan Wysocki, RNC, BSN,
NP; Sharon Myoji Schnare, RN, FNP, CNM, MSN; and
Beth Moran, RN, CN; with the editorial assistance of
Barbara Tchabovsky.*

CHAPTER 4

Brea∫t Cancer ∫creening and Brea∫t Care

Breast cancer is the most common type of cancer among women in the United States, accounting for 30% of all cancers in women. It is the second leading cause of cancer death among women. Currently approximately 43,900 women and 400 men die of breast cancer each year. The morality rate associated with breast cancer has been falling among white women, but not among black women. However, it should be remembered that most—80% to 90%—breast lumps are benign, but risk increases with age. In premenopausal women, 8% of lumps are malignant; in postmenopausal women, 50% are malignant.

Risk Factors for Breast Cancer

- *Increasing Age*—77% of women with a new diagnosis of breast cancer are over 50 years of age. For an 85-year-old woman, the risk is 1 in 8.

- *Family and Personal History*—There are several factors to consider in assessing the family history-risk. If a woman has a first-degree relative—mother, sister, daughter—who had premenopausal bilateral breast cancer, the risk is high, 1 in 5; for a woman with a first-degree relative with premeno-pausal unilateral disease, the risk is1 in 7; and for a woman with a first-degree relative with postmenopausal breast cancer, the risk is 1 in 9.

Risk is also increased for women with abnormal BRCA1 and BRCA2 genes, but it is important to remember that only 5% of breast cancers are linked to these abnormal genes.

A family history of ovarian cancer, colon cancer, or male breast cancer increases risk.

A personal history of previous breast cancer is associated with a 1 in 7 risk of a second tumor.

- *Reproductive History*—Nulliparity and a first pregnancy after age 30 increases risk. A first pregnancy before age 30 decreases risk.

- *Menstrual History*—Menarche before age 12 and menopause after age 55 increases risk. A small increased risk is associated with hormone replacement therapy (HRT). (However, the risk of death from complications of osteoporosis and heart disease without HRT is 30 times higher than the risk of death from breast cancer with HRT.)

- *Environmental Exposure*—Among the environmental factors that increase risk are
  - radiation exposure to the breast during adolescence;
  - smoking, which becomes a significant risk after age 30; and possibly
  - exposure to organochloride pesticides during childhood and adolescence.

- *Other factors*—Other factors that may increase risk include diabetes, obesity, and a diet that

75% of women with newly diagnosed breast cancer have no identifiable risk factors.

includes more than 30% of calories from fat. In addition, alcohol intake is associated with increased risk.

Signs and Symptoms of Breast Cancer

A common sign of breast cancer is a change in the normal architecture and/or appearance of the breast, often detected by the woman herself during a self-breast exam (SBE), by a partner, or by a healthcare provider. The signs include

- a lump;
- a bloody discharge from the nipple;
- sudden redness and pain; and/or
- a dimpling of the skin or *peau d'orange* appearance; or
- ecchymosis

Regional signs such as enlarged lymph nodes may also be found.

Symptoms of breast cancer including breast pain, cough, bone pain, weight loss, fatigue, and anemia may be present in advanced disease.

> *It is important to note that there may be no signs in the breast of cancer.*

Overview of Breast Problems

There are several problems that may be associated with the breast during different times of a woman's life. The following pages briefly discuss major breast problems, outlining their likely time of occurrence, nature, and treatment.

Breast Pain - Mastalgia
Breast pain may be hormonally mediated.

Premenstrual changes increase the volume of the breast and may cause pain in the densest fibrous areas. Cysts and tumors may also cause pain if surrounding tissue is disturbed or regional sensory nerves are stimulated. HRT may potentiate or cause pain in the region.

- ■ *Evaluate*
  - the patient's hormonal status: estrogen/progestin balance

- ■ *Exclude* musculoskeletal problems, such as costochondral syndrome (Tietze's syndrome), a self-limited syndrome, treated with nonsteroidal antiinflammatory drugs (NSAIDs); an overuse syndrome; angina; and hiatal hernia.

- ■ *Intervene to:*
  - Consider use of good supportive bra; diuretic therapy limited to premenstrual interval of symptomatology; or oral contraceptives which suppress symptoms in the majority of mastalgia sufferers.
  - Consider ordering mammography if age appropriate to attenuate patient's possible fear of cancer. However, breast cancer rarely presents with pain.
  - Consider possible tyramine sensitivity, although this is rarely a cause. (In tyramine sensitivity, there is sensitivity to aged cheese, fermented sausages, caviar, dried fish, beer, ale, red wine, sherry, avocados, yeast extracts, bananas, figs, raisins, soy, miso soup, fava beans, ginseng)
  - Many clinicians recommend the following,

Consider the possibility of cancer.
Some cancers present with pain.

---

although there is no scientific data to support the value of these suggestions:

- cessation or lowering of intake of methylxanthines such as caffeine;
- cessation or reduction in smoking and alcohol intake;
- administration of vitamin E 600 to 800 IU/day or evening primrose oil;
- administration of vitamin B complex, 100mg; and selenium, 200mcg;
- use of progesterone cream–Mexican wild yam, 1/4 teaspoon applied to soft breast tissue twice a day for 2-3 weeks a month.

Nipple Discharge (Discharge and Galactorrhea)
In evaluating this complaint, history is very important.

- *Evaluate*
  - the nature of the discharge. Is it milky, multicolored, and sticky; purulent, clear, or watery; yellow or serous; pink or serosanguineous; bloody or sanguineous?
  - if it is truly a discharge or a pseudodischarge that may be associated with trauma, edema, inverted nipples, eczematous lesions, herpes simplex infections, Montgomery gland abscesses, or mammary duct fistulas;
  - if it is spontaneous or induced; and
  - if it is unilateral or bilateral.

If the discharge is bilateral, spontaneous, multiple-duct, and milky, it is most likely galactorrhea.

To manage:

- *Ask about use of any medications, such as tranquilizers, marijuana, or high-estrogen drugs, that may be causing the discharge.*

- *Determine if there is a history of overstimulation of the breast.*

- *Evaluate the volume of the discharge.*

- *Measure prolactin and thyroid levels. Consider ordering computed tomography (CT) or magnetic resonance imaging (MRI) as appropriate in patients with two elevated prolactins and new onset neurological symptoms and in patients with two prolactin levels higher than 50.*

- *Consider possible causes - idiopathic galactorrhea, prolactinoma, Chiari-Frommel Syndrome (microadenoma), thyroid disorders, etc.*

If the discharge is multicolored and sticky, it is usually due to duct ectasia.

A purulent discharge is usually produced by infection, frequently staphylococcal. Treat the infection.

If there is spontaneous bleeding, consider trauma. Examine and observe again after 2 weeks. If still continuing, refer to a specialist.

If there is spontaneous pink or intermittent bloody discharge, refer to a surgeon.

If the discharge is spontaneous single duct, clear or watery, yellow or serous, refer for a ductogram or to a surgeon. Also consider doing a Pap smear of the discharge to rule out malignant cells.

Benign Masses
There are several types of benign masses, including cysts, fibroadenomas, phylloides-type tumors, hamartomas, fat necrosis, and papillomas.

Cysts may be a lifelong occurrence or a hallmark of perimenopause. A cyst is usually a round, smooth, mobile, occasionally fluctuant, mass. It often makes a spontaneous, uncomfortable appearance. It can be reevaluated after menses or aspirated.

A fluid-filled cyst may be aspirated with 22-gauge

needle, after skin prep and local anesthesia. Cloudy, green, or brown fluid is normal. If the fluid is bloody or purulent, the aspirant should be evaluated with cytology. A quickly refilling cyst may be an intracystic papilloma or may be malignant.

A cyst should be evaluated with a mammogram or ultrasound. Ultrasound differentiates solid from cystic lesions and identifies possible suspicious lesions. Multiple cysts in perimenopausal women call for ultrasound and mammograms once a year.

If the cyst is clearly benign and nonpainful, it does not need to be removed. If the cyst is painful or bothersome, aspirate. If the cyst does not disappear with the menstrual cycle, continue to evaluate to exclude a malignant mass. In the presence of a palpable mass, a negative mammogram does not exclude breast carcinoma.

A *milk-filled cyst,* or galactocele, may be aspirated, even if the patient is lactating. Ultrasound may be misleading and call the mass solid. If it is clearly milk-filled, the clinician can wait until the patient finishes breast-feeding to re-aspirate.

Fibroadenomas involve a hyperplasic process involving a terminal ductal lobular unit (TDLU). Increasing size adds connective tissue and other TDLUs. The fibroadenomas usually appear as well-defined, round (usually), rubbery, mobile nodules. They may present as a soft mass with pregnancy and lactation.

This tumor is common in young women 18 to 25 years of age but may also appear at menopause.

Risk Management for NPs:
All unresolved breast masses should be
referred to a surgeon and the referral
carefully documented.

Changes in breast architecture associated with aging may make those previously present tumors palpable. This type of mass is more common among African-American women than among whites.

A fibroadenoma has estrogen and progesterone receptors and may grow with pregnancy and lactation, shrinking afterward.

Ultrasound may be done for diagnostic evaluation and to monitor size. Fine-needle aspiration or core biopsy also provide diagnostic information.

If the fibroadenoma is benign and stable, it need not be removed. If it grows, it should be excised.

A **phylloides-type tumor** is a rare fibroepithelial tumor that is usually benign, rarely malignant (cytosarcoma phylloides). It is a painless, smooth, round, and multimodular mass. It should be evaluated with a mammogram and ultrasound and the patient referred to a surgeon for excision.

A **hamartoma** is a fibroadenolipoma and fat that appear as a well circumscribed, soft, mobile mass. It should be evaluated with a mammogram and the patient referred to a surgeon for excision.

A **fat necrosis** is a lump appearing after trauma or surgery. A fat necrosis may vary in size and possibly be tender. Evaluate with a mammogram and ultrasound.

A **papilloma** occurs in large ducts. Peripheral lesions are usually multiple. The papilloma produces clear to hemorrhagic discharge. A ductogram is helpful in diagnosis. Papillomas are associated with an increased risk of cancer.

Infections
There are several types of infections that can affect the breast.

Mastitis is an inflammation of breast tissue caused by an infection. It is most common in breast-feeding mothers, but it can occur in non-lactating women.

The breast becomes painful, warm, and red, and chills and fever usually occur. Treatment with antibiotics is indicated with penicillinase-resistant antibiotics (such as dicloxacillin). If symptoms are severe, patient may require intravenous antibiotics. Abscesses must be treated by surgical drainage. The patient can continue to breast-feed or manually empty her breast.

Breast Abscesses occur when the central cavity fills with neutrophils and necrotic debris. Adjacent tissues undergo inflammatory changes that eventually lead to fibrosis.

In a lactational abscess, there is pain, a red hot mass, and chills and fever. Treat with antibiotics (Duricef 500 b.i.d. or Keflex 500 q.i.d.) If fluctuant mass, aspirate or refer for treatment

A non-lactational abscess is more common in smokers than in nonsmokers. If it is a peripheral abscess, aspirate, culture, and treat with an antibiotic. If it is a subareolar breast abscess, aspirate if fluctuant, culture, and give antibiotics. These abscesses tend to recur, and surgery may be needed. In non-lactating women, differential diagnosis should include consideration of chronic infection, carcinoma, tuberculosis, an inflamed cyst, and duct ectasia.

Lymphadenopathy
Lymphadenopathy can be benign, resulting from infection, reaction to an antiperspirant, a cat scratch, or Lyme's disease. It can also be malignant, associated with breast cancer, Hodgkin's disease, lymphoma.

Mondor's Disease
Mondor's Disease involves a superficial thrombophlebitis of the thoracoabdominal vein, resulting in a tender cordlike structure. Treat with NSAIDs, moist heat, and reassurance. The disease usually resolves spontaneously in 2 to 10 weeks.

Evaluation of a Breast Lump

The evaluation of any breast mass or other breast problem involves several steps. The following provides a detailed approach to such an evaluation in the primary care setting.

Complete History

Include in the history:

- *menstrual history;*
- *use of medication including over-the-counter (OTCs) drugs and herbal remedies;*
- *known allergies;*
- *family history;*
- *medical history;*
- *recent emotional stress; and*
- *detailed history of presenting problem, particularly questions concerning any change in the mass.*

Physical Examination

- *Examine from the opposite side of the table to the breast you are going to palpate.*
- *Perform a thorough exam of each breast, from clavicle to below the breast, mid-axillary line to mid-sternum, axillary nodes, and supra/infraclavicular nodes.*
- *Identify normal architectural pattern.*
  - upper outer quadrant fibroglandular tissue, possible central area of fibroglandular tissue; fibroglandular tissue may also extend across upper outer quadrant and upper inner quadrant;
  - lower edge of breast may be nodular, like a pebbly river bed, increasing with age; inframammary ridge identification;
  - hollow under nipple;

- *Rock the hand over the breast starting in upper outer quadrant.*

  - Feel with the fingers and lateral palm of hand.

  - Discern gross architecture.

  - Examine the whole breast in grid fashion.

  - Use both hands to feel

- *Using fingers from proximal to the DIP joint, roll the fingers over the breast tissue, again in grid pattern.*

  - Feel the tissue between the fingers and the ribs.

  - Normal breast tissue changes its shape with this movement. A lump does not.

- *Use fingers to evaluate nodules or masses for size, shape, consistency, mobility, and tenderness.*

- *Palpate areola and nipple. Do not squeeze. Pressure from exam should be enough to express a discharge if present.*

- *Examine axillary nodes while patient is sitting.*

  - With patient's arm relaxed, place hand with fingertip touching the trapezius muscle posteriorly.

  - Pull fingers forward to just past the anterior axillary line.

  - Start high in the axilla and move down the ribs

  - Palpate the tail of the breast and the pectoral muscle

- *Inspect skin for dimpling, vascularity, erythema, or lesions*

Alternative Suggestions for Preventing

Many nurse practitioners and other clinicians recommend
several measures to help a woman reduce her chances of
developing breast masses and/or breast cancer. The following
list includes some of the suggestions sometimes given.
However, it should be remembered that the value of these
suggestions has not been documented by scientific data.

- Reduce exposure to unopposed estradiol by
  decreasing amount of dairy and other fat in the diet;
  decreasing intake of alcohol; decreasing sugar

Diagnostic Imaging for Palpable Abnormality

- *Mammogram if patient is over 30 years of age.
  If abnormality is suspicious for malignancy,
  order mammogram if patient is over 25 years
  old. Remember that a young breast may be
  dense and this can lead to a decreased ability to
  identify a lesion and that mammograms are
  usually not done in women younger than 25
  years. Continue workup even if abnormality is
  not visible on mammogram.*

- *Ultrasound using High Resolution Imaging to
  further evaluate a lump. This is valuable for
  lesions not seen on a mammogram but
  palpable. It can differentiate solid from cystic
  masses and provide an indicator of malignancy.
  Good tool for evaluation of young women*

Mammographic Lesions (not palpable)

- *Evaluate mass, architectural distortion, or
  calcification on film*

- *Stereotactic biopsy—Core biopsy gives a tissue
  diagnosis with good accuracy. No
  hospitalization, anesthesia, or surgery*

- *If lesion is visible on ultrasound, use*

    consumption (sugar is converted to fat in the body); increasing phytoestrogens in the diet by adding soy products such as miso, tofu, soy milk, soy powders to the diet; and increasing fiber in the diet to help increase elimination of circulating estrogens.

- Stop smoking
- Increase intake of vitamins C, B and of selenium and other antioxidants to help clear the body of free radicals.

    ultrasound-guided core biopsy. This is more cost effective

- *Refer to surgeon as indicated*

Tissue Sampling of Palpable Mass
In the primary care setting, the clinician may

- *for a cyst, perform a fine-needle aspiration (FNA). Refer to a specialist if no fluid is obtained.*
- *for a fibroadenoma, perform a fine-needle aspiration or core biopsy.*
- *for a suspicious mass, do a fine-needle aspiration or core biopsy or refer.*

> *Only perform FNAs or core biopsy if proficient. Otherwise refer to a surgeon.*

The author of this chapter, Fiona Shannon, ARNP, MHS, FNP, is in private practice in Kingston, Washington.

Breast exam technique developed by Diane Jones, MD, Seattle, WA.

NOTES

Substance Abuse: The Hidden Disease

Background on Addiction

Addiction is a disease: It is a pathological illness derived from a relationship with mood-altering chemicals resulting in dysfunctional behavior. Addiction is a primary disease of the brain. It is not caused by irresponsible use of drugs or alcohol. It is not the result of stress; nor is it a matter of will.

Addiction embraces a series of biochemical reactions in the brain, some of which are irreversible. Once the "biochemical switch" in the brain is turned on, the brain is never the same again. That's why we talk about people being in recovery. Addiction is a process which continues without cure—but with containment.

How Does Addiction Occur?

Addiction is a process, not an event. The onset of the process often is not acute. It is a subtle process, as are the behavior changes that accompany addiction. One old adage is: Use, abuse, addiction.

Not everyone who uses alcohol or drugs becomes addicted. However, the more you use the substance, the better your chances for moving toward addiction.

Abuse is the repeated overuse of alcohol or drugs. In the use and abuse stages of addiction, the person retains the ability to choose to use the drug or alcohol. In the next stage—the addictive phase of the disease—the ability to choose is no longer available. The use of drugs or alcohol has changed the chemicals in the brain, often permanently, and need and craving replace choice. Addiction has occurred at this point.

Characteristics of Addicts

Attributes of addicts include:

- excessive, compulsive use of the substance ("I use/drink too much because I need to use/drink too much.");

- the experience of harmful consequences ("I use/drink too much and drive impaired.");

- repetition ("I use despite warning signals.");

- intentions to stop ("I resolve not to drink/use, and then I break my resolutions.");

- denial ("I don't have a problem; you are over-reacting.");

- gradual deterioration on all levels ("My work record has declined; my friends have changed; my family doesn't understand me.")

Abnormal Patterns of Use

The way in which a person uses their chemical of choice reflects aberrant choices. These include:

- preoccupation with alcohol or drugs or with the next opportunity to use them;

- increased tolerance to alcohol or the drug— the person uses the substance more than anyone else and often functions acceptably;

- gulping drinks or using other drugs quickly to "get started";

- drinking or using alone and tending to isolate himself or herself when using the chemical of choice, even if it's in a bar or at a party;

- use of alcohol or drugs as medicine for relief of

tension or anxiety or as an aid to sleep;

- blackouts—cannot remember events, action, behavior after drinking or using; may occur after heavy drinking or using, but can also occur with only small amounts;

- secluded stash—hiding alcohol or drug supplies in various locations so the next drink or fix is always near by;

- non-premeditated drinking—drinking or using more than planned; finding excuses to continue to have more than planned.

Suspicious Actions of Substance Abusers—Red Flags

Some red flags to help identify substance-abusing patients include patients who

- frequently miss appointments;

- frequently request written excuses for work;

- present with chief complaints of insomnia, bad nerves, or vague pain;

- appear depressed, agitated, or have difficulty making eye contact;

- often lose prescriptions and request refills for pain pills or tranquilizers;

- often have many accidents, falls, or burns, or are in frequent fights;

- have a history of gastrointestinal (GI) bleeds, peptic ulcers, pancreatitis, cellulitis, complicated pregnancies, multiple abortions, or sexually transmitted diseases;

- have high-risk sexual behaviors;

- have a family history of addiction;

- have a history of childhood sexual, physical, or emotional abuse;
- have a history of repeated marital problems and/or have custody issues with children.

Assessment

The first task in the assessment process is to monitor the denial of the individual. Denial is the hallmark of an addiction. Denial is the person's inability to connect herself or himself to the disease. Additionally, family members often don't want to face the truth about a loved one's addiction. As bad as it is, sometimes the chaos created by the addiction is comfortable because everyone knows what to expect.

In assessing chemically dependent individuals, one must consider the physiological, sociological, and psychological factors. Physiological signs are found in the history and physical: look for abnormal liver enzymes, anemias, tremors, ulcers, gynecomastia, ascites. Sociological factors determine not only whether people will drink/use, but how they will view themselves after drinking/using. The psychological factors are the emotions or feelings and the personality of the individual. Mental obsessions, emotional compulsions, poor self image, and negative attitudes can be important indicators of substance abuse.

Assessment is a process, just like addiction is. It is the picture of the individual at a specific time. Just as a picture reflects the image, so an assessment reflects a spot on the continuum of the person's disease. Often red flags are raised during routine histories and physical examinations or brief visits because you sense something in the behavior or signs and symptoms. Your "gut feeling" is often accurate.

The first step is an initial screen. Using the CAGE questionnaire, interject the following questions into your patient history:

C = cutdown. Have you ever tried to cut down on your drinking or drug use?

A = annoyed. Has anyone ever been annoyed with your drinking or drug use?

G = guilty. Have you ever felt guilty about your drinking or drug use?

E = eye-opener. Have you ever taken a drink to get you started? (Remember, eye openers are not limited just to morning drinking. Often dysfunctional drinking begins at "happy hour.")

The initial screening questions should also include questions regarding trauma. Ask about fractures, accidents, head injuries, fights with and without alcohol/drugs. Find out if the trauma occurred as a result of someone else's use of alcohol or drugs. Violence, especially against women, often occurs while a person is under the influence of alcohol or other drugs. Use the questions in the initial screen in every history you take. Because of the denial factor, sliding into questions is easier than confronting difficult questions directly.

The next level of assessment is the screening test. Two excellent sources are the MAST test and the National Institute on Alcohol Abuse and Alcoholism (NIAAA) Screening and Brief Intervention Procedures. The screening test is administered after a discussion has taken place on the use and abuse of alcohol and drugs. It is an effective tool to confront denial. It gives the patient the opportunity to actually see how alcohol and drug have affected his/her life. (See MAST on pages 90-91.)

After Assessment: What To Do?

How do you handle the information a patient gives you? The general rule of thumb is to go slowly and gently. Don't think you can solve a person's problems in one visit. Prioritize their problems. Identify the

M A S T - G *

Directions: The following is a list of questions about your past and present drinking habits. Please answer yes or no to each question by marking the line next to the question. When you are finished answering the questions please add up how many "yes" responses you checked and put that number in the space provided at the end.

YES (1) NO (2)

After drinking have you ever noticed an increase in your heart rate or a beating in your chest?   ____   ____

When talking with others, do you ever underestimate how much you actually drink?   ____   ____

Does alcohol make you sleepy so that you often fall asleep in your chair?   ____   ____

After a few drinks, have you sometimes not eaten or been able to skip a meal because you didn't feel hungry?   ____   ____

Does having a few drinks help decrease your shakiness or tremors?   ____   ____

Does alcohol sometimes make it hard for you to remember parts of the day or night?   ____   ____

Do you have rules for yourself that you won't drink before a certain time of the day?   ____   ____

Have you lost interest in hobbies or activities you used to enjoy?   ____   ____

When you wake up in the morning, do you ever have trouble remembering part of the night before?   ____   ____

Does having a drink help you sleep?   ____   ____

Do you hide your alcohol bottles from family members?   ____   ____

After a social gathering, have you ever felt embarrassed because you drank too much? ____ ____

Have you ever been concerned that drinking might be harmful to your health? ____ ____

Do you like to end an evening with a night-cap? ____ ____

Did you find your drinking increased after someone close to you died? ____ ____

In general, would you prefer to have a few drinks at home rather than go out to social events? ____ ____

Are you drinking more now than in the past? ____ ____

Do you usually take a drink to relax or calm your nerves? ____ ____

Do you drink to take your mind off your problems? ____ ____

Have you ever increased your drinking after experiencing a loss in your life? ____ ____

Do you sometimes drive when you have had too much to drink? ____ ____

Has a doctor or nurse ever said they were worried or concerned about your drinking? ____ ____

Have you ever made rules to manage your drinking? ____ ____

When you feel lonely does having a drink help? ____ ____

TOTAL "YES" response ____

Scoring: 5 or more "yes" responses is indicative of alcohol problem.

*Reprinted from The American Journal for Nurse Practitioners, June 1998, page 29.

ones you can handle; refer those that are out of your area of expertise to others who are more qualified. Your role is to identify the presence of a problem. Your next job is to refer to a professional skilled in diagnosing this disease. The diagnosis actually confirms what the patient already knows in his/her own heart—but is too scared to admit. Your role as a screener frees you from the role of provider of treatment. Your role is to introduce the subject to the patient and recommend behavior changes. These behavior changes are: abstinence, attendance at 12 Step support groups, and evaluation by a healthcare provider experienced in dealing with addiction. It is very important that you maintain your boundaries and your goals for each person.

Treatment

Treatment for addicted patients involves changing behavior. To change one's behavior, all aspects of the person must be examined, scrutinized, and explored. This includes the spiritual, emotional, physical, and mental parts of an individual.

Treatment involves two areas: treatment for the impaired person and treatment for the family. Treatment modalities available for the impaired person include inpatient, outpatient, and self-help groups and programs, as well as combinations of all. Equally important is treatment for the family. The spouse or the significant other and children of the addict must be treated, as they suffer from their own disease as a result of the illness of the addict. Treatment for them comes in the form of self-help groups and psychotherapy. Family therapy is essential to the recovery of both the impaired person and family members.

Treatment is a process. It is not easy, and it is not without failures. Recovery is a way of life. It is the re-building of a life that has been shattered and torn in every area.

Relapse can occur at any time in the process, and special care must be given to ensure progress. Relapse is not just the act of taking a drink or drug. It is the return to behavior patterns and to the thought processes that are destructive to the individual. Relapse is process too, just as addiction is. It culminates in the action of the chemical, but it began long before that event. Relapse prevention needs to be taught to both the addict and the family early in the recovery phase. For some, relapse can signal death. For others, relapse can be viewed as an acknowledgment of destructive behavior. It can serve as the springboard to greater understanding of the disease process.

A Few Words About Women

Women often hide their drinking better than men, and this leaves women the sad opportunity to stay in their addiction longer before they receive help. The stigma of being a female addict is real and considerable. Women often use prescription drugs as a way to hide their chemical-taking behavior. Prescription drugs are not obvious, and they are prescribed *for* the patient. This inflames the role of denial in the additive process.

Childhood incest is a common problem among female alcoholics. Incest is a very, very long-lived and well-suppressed secret. Alcoholic women not only experience more sexual abuse than their non-alcoholic counterparts, but the nature of the abuse experience is often more violent and more frequent, involves more perpetrators, and continues for a longer duration.

Identification and assessment of women addicts are life-saving measures for women, their children, and their other family members.

The author of this chapter, Kate Malliarakis, CNP, MSM, NCADC2, is a nurse practitioner who is a National Certified Alcohol and Drug Counselor, Level 2 (NCADC2). She is Chief of Specific Drugs and Special Programs Branch, Office of Demand Reduction, Office of National Drug Control Policy, Washington, D.C.

NOTES

CHAPTER 5

Managing Your Practice

Practice Issues

Whatever a nurse practitioner's (NP's) particular area of expertise, there are some issues that are relevant to NPs in general. These issues include:

- *legal scope of practice;*
- *necessity of physician collaboration;*
- *qualification differences, state-to-state;*
- *credentialing; and*
- *reimbursement provisions specific to NPs.*

Scope of Practice—Scope of practice varies from state to state. For example, in Oregon, scope of practice is defined specifically, as follows:

> *"The nurse practitioner is independently responsible and accountable for the continuous and comprehensive management of a broad range of health care, which may include:*

- promotion and maintenance of health;

- prevention of illness and disability;

- assessment of clients, synthesis and analysis of data, and application of nursing principles and therapeutic modalities;

- management of health care during acute and chronic phases of illness;

- admission of his/her clients to hospitals and long-term care facilities and management of client care in these facilities;

- counseling;

- consultation and/or collaboration with other care providers and community resources;

- referral to other health care providers and community resources;

- management and coordination of care;

- use of research skills;

- diagnosis of health/illness status; and

- prescription and/or administration of therapeutic devices and measures, including legend drugs and controlled substances consistent with the practitioner's specialty category and scope of practice.

The nurse practitioner is responsible for recognizing limits of knowledge and experience, and for resolving situations beyond his/her nurse practitioner expertise by consulting with or referring clients to other health care providers."
(Oregon Administrative Rules 851-050-0005)

In South Carolina, however, scope of practice is defined rather vaguely as follows

The Nurse Practitioner, Clinical Nurse Specialist functioning in the extended role, or Certified Registered Nurse Anesthetist is subject, at all times, to the scope and standards or practice established by the nationally recognized credentialing organization representing the specialty area of practice, and must function within the scope of practice of the South Carolina Nurse Practice Act and shall not be in violation of the South Carolina Medical Practice Act. The scope and standards of practice for each specialty area of nursing practice shall be on file in the Board office and available upon request. (South Carolina Nursing Regulations: Section 91-6.)

The "Expanded Role" of the registered nurse means a process of diffusion and implies multi-directional change. Expansion, as a process of role change, is undertaken not only to fill perceived needs in the healthcare system, but also to project new components or systems of health care. The authority base for practice from which the expanded role emanates is the body of knowledge that constitutes the nurse's preparation for practice. The expanded role requires specialized knowledge, judgment, and skill, but does not require nor permit medical diagnosis or medical prescription of therapeutic or corrective measures. (South Carolina Nursing Regulations §91-3)

In Washington, scope of practice is defined broadly but generally, as follows:

Advanced registered nurse practitioners function within the scope of practice reviewed and approved by the board. Those scopes reviewed are the statements of scope accepted by the certifying bodies as the basis for their test plan and selection of test items. Advanced registered nurse practitioners are qualified to assume primary responsibility for the care of their patients. The practice incorporates the use of independent judgment as well as collaborative interaction with other health care professionals when indicated

> *in the assessment and management of*
> *wellness and conditions as appropriate to*
> *the advanced registered nurse*
> *practitioner's area of specialization.*
> (Washington Administrative Code 246-839-300).

NPs should review the language of their state law regarding scope of practice.

Physician Collaboration—Necessity of physician collaboration also varies greatly from state to state. For example, in Oregon, six other states, and the District of Columbia, no physician collaboration is required by law. In four states, all NP activities are legally the delegated activities of a physician. In nine states, NPs must be supervised by a physician. In 23 states, NPs practice in collaborative agreements with physicians.

Qualifications—Qualifications for NPs also differ from state to state. In 18 states, a master's degree is required. In 30 states, certification by a national certifying agency is required. In Nevada, NPs must pass an exam on Nevada law.

Credentialing—Credentialing requirements differ somewhat among various hospitals and managed care organizations (MCOs). In general, the credentialing applications mirror physicians' applications, with the omission of a residency and medical school. Nurse practitioners should be aware that unanswered or incomplete answers to credentialing questions can affect admission to provider panels, and ultimately the ability to practice and be reimbursed.

Reimbursement—Reimbursement provisions specific to NPs come in the form of federal law, state law, and local policies of insurers and managed care organizations. Some state laws specifically designate NPs as primary care providers (PCPs). Some state laws require certain insurers to reimburse for NP services. Some states neither provide for NP reimbursement nor designate NPs as PCPs.

A nurse practitioner who is self-employed or the employer of a nurse practitioner should consult state law before attempting to bill for NP services. Likewise, those wishing to bill for NP services should inquire about the policies of local insurance companies and managed care organizations regarding reimbursement of NP services and NP provider panel status.

Types of Practice

While an NP may assume that state law regarding scope of practice controls an NP's ability to perform healthcare services, there are a number of other laws which may also govern an NP's ability to practice. For example, a body of law may govern hospitals and may or may not address the role of NPs. Federal law governing hospitals does not address nurse practitioners. It does, however, provide that the care of hospital patients be overseen by a physician and gives physicians the authority to delegate to other healthcare providers.

State law may or may not address NP practice in nursing homes, hospice centers, residential treatment centers, correctional facilities, and schools. Unless NP practice is specifically authorized in a setting, an NP working in a setting may find that administrators or government auditors may question or challenge the NP's authority to order care or medications or document in the patient's medical record.

Negotiating Salary

Some employers have a salary scale for nurse practitioners, with minimal leeway for negotiation and minimal potential for negotiation. Others, however, are open to negotiation.

One method of confronting salary negotiations is to focus on hard figures which document an NP's monetary contribution to a practice and the costs of an NP to a practice.

NPs bring in income on a fee-for-service basis or on a per-member-per-month basis. Figuring an NP's share of income in a fee-for-service practice is done by multiplying the number of visits by the fee collected per visit. When a practice's patients are capitated, an NP's share of income is figured by multiplying the number of patients on an NP's panel by the per-member-per-month fee coming into the practice.

The cost of maintaining an NP is figured by adding practice expenses and the cost of physician consultation. Practice expenses can be estimated or calculated for a particular practice. For a solo practice, expenses can be 40% to 50% of income. For a large practice, expenses are lower—20% to 30% of income. Practice expenses include rent, salaries, taxes and benefits of support staff, taxes and benefits of NPs, supplies, laboratory expenses, depreciation, car, continuing education, and insurance (malpractice, worker's compensation, and premises insurance).

An NP who needs a great deal of physician consultation should expect to compensate the NP's employer physicians for their time. An NP who needs little consultation should command a higher salary, because he or she needs little of a physician's time. Until NPs no longer need a physician on written agreement, all NPs should expect to pay something for physician consultation. Experienced NPs often pay physician employers/consultants 10% to 15% of their net income brought into the practice.

Most employers will want a percentage of an NP's earnings as profit. An experienced NP who needs little consultation from an employer physician might consider his or her contribution to profit to be the 10% to 15% of net income paid for consultation as noted in the paragraph above. A newer NP should expect to contribute 10% to 15% of net earnings to an employer as profit, in addition to 15% to 25% of net earnings for physician consultation.

To project an appropriate salary for a particular NP:

1. calculate income to the practice based on NP billings;

2. subtract 10% for unpaid bills;

3. subtract

   a. the calculated figure for practice expenses (20% to 50% of earnings),

   b. the cost of physician consultation (10% to 20% of net earnings), and

   c. a percentage for employer profit.

Fee-for-Service Practices—In a fee-for-service practice, an NP who sees fifteen patients per day at $35 per patient visit, on average, brings in $525 per day. Allowing for one week off for continuing education, one week off for illness, and four weeks off for vacation, this NP will bring in $120,750 a year, potentially. But not all bills are paid. With a 90% collection rate—a reasonable collection rate for an efficient practice—this NP actually will bring in $108,675 per year.

An NP who sees twenty-four patients per day will bring in $840 per day, or $193,200 per year in accounts receivable. With a 90% collection rate, this NP will bring $173,880 to the practice.

Deducting 40% of the NP's gross generated income for overhead expenses (rent, benefits, continuing education, supplies, malpractice, lab expenses, and depreciation of equipment) leaves $65,205 for the 15-patient-per-day NP and $104,328 for the 24-patient-per-day NP.

Further deducting 15% of that figure to pay a physician for consultation services leaves $55,425 in salary for the 15-patient-per-day NP and $88,679 in salary for the 24-patient-per-day NP.

Deducting 10% for employer profit leaves $49,882 in salary for the 15-patient-per-day NP and $79,811 for the 24-patient-per-day NP.

Capitated Practices—In a fully capitated practice, an NP who has a panel of 1000 patients at an average fee per-member-per-month of $10 will bring in $120,000 annually. There should be a 100% collection rate under a capitated system of reimbursement.

Applying 40% to overhead leaves $72,000, and paying 15% for physician consultation and 10% for employer profit leaves $55,080 for the NP salary. An NP with a larger panel will make more.

An NP embarking on a salary negotiation needs to gather the following data from the employer:

1. What is the most frequently billed CPT code for the practice? What amount does the practice bill and receive, on average, for that CPT code?

2. What is the percent of practice income that goes to cover practice expenses? If the employer will not reveal that information, ask how many providers share practice overhead expenses. A solo practitioner pays 43% of income for office expenses, whereas a practice of 10 to 24 doctors pays 23.5% for office expenses. Determine the appropriate rate to deduct for practice expenses.

3. What is the collection rate for the practice. Remember, 90% is good.

4. How many patients is the NP expected to see per day?

Then, an NP needs to make the following assessments about his or her speed and comfort level:

1. How many patients can I see per hour, day, month, and year?

2. How much physician consultation time will I need—a 10-minute consultation on every patient, a 5-minute consultation once a day, or a 5-minute consultation once a year?

The New NP—A newly graduated NP without experience may be able to see only ten patients a day, with four or five 10-minute physician consultations per day, for the first 6 months. Plugging in the figures as in the examples above, the NP will bill 2400 visits per year (two weeks vacation for the new grad) at $35 per visit to total $84,000 in accounts receivable. With a 90% collection rate, the new NP will bring in $75,600. Deduct 40% for practice expenses, which brings the net income to $45,360.

Because a new NP often requires significant consultation time with a physician (or experienced NP), deduct 25% ($11,340) for payment for consultation, bringing the NP salary down to $34,020. With a contribution to employer profit, this new NP's appropriate salary is down to $30,618.

After 6 months, when the same NP becomes more comfortable and more efficient, the income numbers should double, and consultation requirements should decrease, so that the appropriate salary would more closely approximate the salary of the 15-patient-per-day NP, and, eventually the 24-patient-per-day NP, used in the examples above. Many employers start a new NP at a salary significantly higher than $30,618, expecting that low productivity in the first 6 months will be balanced by high productivity in the second 6 months.

The Experienced NP—Experienced NPs who are seeing more than fifteen patients per day at CPT code level 99213 or higher should be making least $50,000 per year. If not, there are inefficiencies in the practice, or the NP is not sharing in the profits.

Other Factors Affecting Salary Negotiations—Several other factors affect salary negotiation—the collection rate for the practice, the administrative duties handled by the NP, benefits, and willingness of insurers to reimburse for NP services.

Collection rate for the practice—Some practices collect a high percentage of billings and some practices have poor rates of collections. A good collections rate is 90% of billings. A poor collections rate is 50% of billings. The matter is further complicated in that some insurers are waiting 90-120 days before paying bills. A practice which accounts for an unpaid bill as a bad debt after 90 days may have a lower rate of collections than a practice which has a different system of accounting.

An NP should not be subsidizing a practice with a low rate of collections by accepting a low salary. If an NP is negotiating salary based on collected billings, the NP should obtain information from the practice manager about the practice's collection rate. If the rate of collection is low (less than 75%), the NP should negotiate a salary which takes into account the NP's billings, rather than the practice's collected billings.

Administrative duties handled by the nurse practitioner—An NP who handles policy-writing; management of practice personnel; or ordering, marketing, or negotiating for a practice can expect a higher salary than a nurse practitioner who handles no additional duties. The NP and employer should agree upon the administrative duties which the NP will handle and then assign a monetary value to those duties.

Benefits—Employers pay taxes on each employee. Every employer must pay one-half of employees' Medicare and Social Security taxes and all of each employee's worker's compensation and unemployment insurance. Those costs alone are about 12% of wages. With each additional benefit the costs to the employer rise.

Employers commonly offer NPs some or all of the following benefits:

- *health insurance,*
- *paid sick time,*
- *paid vacation, and*
- *retirement plan.*

Some employers also pay the following business expenses for NPs:

- *continuing education,*
- *professional association dues,*
- *license fees,*
- *journal subscriptions,*
- *car allowance, and*
- *cellular telephone and/or beeper.*

Benefits can easily be 25% of salary. An NP who wants or needs a wide variety of benefits might expect less salary than an NP who is willing to decline benefits.

NPs should also be aware that physicians often receive a more extensive benefits package than nurse practitioners. While benefits for a nurse practitioner may run at 25% of salary, benefits for a physician may run at 35% of salary.

Willingness of insurers to reimburse for NP services—As a business matter, NPs working in states where NP services are not reimbursed can demand less salary than can NPs in states where NP services are reimbursed, in states where NPs can achieve the designation primary care provider (PCP) from managed care organizations, and in states in which NPs can admit patients to hospitals.

Reimbursement rates—Where payers reimburse NPs at the same rates as physician, NPs can negotiate better salaries than in states where payers reimburse NPs at a lower rate.

Reimbursement

Rate for NP Services—Some insurers pay the same rate for nurse practitioner services as they do for physician services. Others pay 85% or some other percentage. Reimbursement for patients covered by Medicaid is 100% of the physician's rate in some states, 70% in other states.

Payers—There are six sources of reimbursement for NP services:

1. *Medicare:* a federal health insurance program for the elderly and disabled;

2. *Medicaid:* a health insurance program funded by the federal government, administered by the states, for mothers and children below the poverty line, and other individuals who have short-term disabilities;

3. *Indemnity insurers:* companies which, in return for premiums paid by employers or individuals, pay each charge of providers for health care given to the insured;

4. *Managed care organizations:* companies which, in return for premiums paid by employers or by individuals, pay for the health care of the insured individuals, through a variety of payment mechanisms which may include fee-for-service or capitated payments;

5. *Contracts:* companies which pay for specific health services by contract, with payments dependent upon the terms of the contract; and

6. *Patients:* patients paying their own bills, according to a fee schedule determined by the providers, and perhaps negotiated with the patient.

Getting Paid—For each payer, there is a mechanism for reimbursement. Briefly, those mechanisms are:

- *Medicare*—Apply to the local Medicare carrier for a provider number. If a patient covered by Medicare is enrolled in a managed care plan, the clinician must apply to the managed care organization for provider status. If a patient is not enrolled in managed care, the clinician submits bills for services rendered to the local Medicare carrier, on a Health Care Financing Administration (HCFA) 1500 form. HCFA 1500 forms may be purchased from the American Medical Association at 1-800-621-8335.

- *Medicaid*—Clinicians apply to the state Medicaid agency for provider numbers. If a patient is enrolled in a managed care organization, the clinician must apply to the managed care organization for provider status. If a patient is not enrolled in managed care, the clinician submits bills for services rendered to the state Medicaid agency on a HCFA 1500 form.

- *Indemnity insurers*—Some indemnity insurers, such as Blue Cross/Blue Shield, require clinicians to apply for provider numbers. Others do not. Billing personnel should know the policies of each indemnity insurer. Usually, insurers accept the HCFA 1500 billing form.

- *Managed care organizations*—In order to be reimbursed, clinicians must be admitted to the provider panel for each managed care organization. Admission involves application, passing a credentialing screen, and, usually, negotiating and signing a contract specifying what services will be provided, the conditions of participation with the managed care organization, and the reimbursement system to be used.

- *Contracts*—Clinicians may negotiate to provide specific services for an agency or business for a set fee or on a fee-for-service basis.

■ *Patients*—Clinicians develop a fee schedule for each type of visit or procedure. Patients pay their bills, at the time of service, by credit card or on a payment schedule.

Glossary

Common terms used in billing include:

CPT Code: Current Procedural Terminology, a uniform coding system developed by the American Medical Association and adopted by third-party payers for use in claim submission.

ICD-9: International Classification of Diseases, 9th revision. The classification of disease by medical diagnosis, codified into 6-digit numbers.

Incident to services: The full term is "incident to a physician's professional service." A Medicare term, meaning services furnished as an "integral, although incidental, part of the physician's personal professional services in the course of diagnosis or treatment of an injury or illness." To qualify under this definition, the services of non-physicians must be rendered under a physician's "direct personal supervision." Non-physicians must be employees of a physician or physician group. Services must be furnished during a course of treatment where a physician performs an initial service and subsequent services of a frequency which reflect the physician's active participation in and management of a course of treatment. Direct personal supervision in the office setting does not mean that a physician must be in the same room. However, a physician must be present in the office suite and immediately available to provide assistance and direction throughout the time a nurse practitioner is performing services.

Medicare: A federal program administered nationally by the Health Care Finance Administration (HCFA) and administered locally by Medicare carrier agencies. Medicare covers patients who are 65 years and older who have enrolled and pay premiums and disabled individuals who qualify for Social Security disability payments and benefits.

Medicaid: A federal program, administered by the states, for mothers and children who qualify on the basis of poverty, and for adults who are disabled for the short-term—for 1 year or less—and who qualify on the basis of poverty.

Usual and customary: An insurance industry term for a charge which 1) is usual and customary when compared with the charges made for similar services and supplies; and which 2) is made to persons having similar medical conditions in the county of residence of the policyholder or such larger area than a county as needed to secure a representative cross section of fees.

Common terms used in managed care include:

Capitation: A fee paid by an HMO to a healthcare provider, per patient, per month, for care of an HMO member. Capitated fees for primary care run between $5 and $35 per member per month, based on a patient's age and sex.

Fee-for-service: Reimbursement for healthcare services under a fee schedule. Fees are based on a complex variety of factors, including the number and type of services provided, the CPT and ICD-9 codes, the geographic area of service, and certain expenses of the provider.

Health Maintenance Organization (HMO): A prepaid, comprehensive system of health benefits which combines the financing and delivery of health services to subscribers. HMOs may pay providers on a fee-for-service basis or on a capitated basis. HMOs limit the providers they deal with to those on their "panel."

Indemnity insurer: An insurance company that pays for the medical care of its insured but which does not deliver health care.

Managed Care Organization (MCO): An insurer which provides both healthcare services and payment for the services. It is in contrast to indemnity insurers, which pay for, but do not provide, healthcare services. MCO is an umbrella term, which may include health maintenance organizations (HMOs), provider-sponsored organizations (PSOs), or physician-hospital organizations (PHOs).

NCQA: The National Committee on Quality Assurance (NCQA), a non-profit, consumer-oriented group which rates managed care organizations on quality of care and sells the rating data to employers who purchase health plan services.

Reimbursement: Payment for medical services already delivered.

Third-party payer: An insurance company, health maintenance organization (HMO), or government agency which pays for medical services for a patient.

The author of this chapter, Carolyn Buppert, JD, CRNP, is an attorney specializing in healthcare issues and a practicing NP in the Baltimore, MD area.

CHAPTER 6
Legal Issues in Providing Health Care

Risk Assessment

A person who is being abused may have little opportunity to talk about it. Clinicians who provide patients that opportunity will find that a surprising number of patients will reveal that they have been or are being physically abused. Clinicians must then decide whether the patient is in immediate danger, and if so, plan an intervention to protect the patient's safety.

Two questions, added to a health history, can help the clinician quickly assess a patient's risk. Ask:

Has anyone been hurting you?

Do you feel safe?

Assuming that all women are at risk for abuse, a nurse practitioner may find that a policy of counseling all women about how to avoid abusive incidents is sound. For example, a clinician might have a handout for teenagers explaining which relations with the opposite sex are appropriate for their age, what situations—alcohol consumption, unsupervised visiting—can lead to unwanted sexual relations, and how to firmly decline sexual advances. Signs listing resources for victims of abuse and hotline numbers may be posted in the waiting rooms.

Sexual Abuse

Involving Minors—Sexual abuse is defined by state law and varies from state to state. For example, a Maine statute defines the crime of sexual abuse as follows:

A person is guilty of sexual abuse of a minor if:

A. Having attained the age of 19 years, the person engages in a sexual act with another person, not the actor's spouse, who has attained the age of 14 years but has not attained the age of 16 years, provided that the actor is at least 5 years older than the other person; or...

C. Having attained the age of 21 years, the person who has attained the age of 16 years but not the age of 18 years, and is a student enrolled in a private or public elementary, secondary or special education school, facility, or institution and the actor is a teacher, employee, or other official in the school district, school union, educational unit, school facility, or institution in which the student is enrolled.

It is a defense to a prosecution under subsection 1, paragraph A, that the actor reasonably believed the other person to have attained his 16th birthday. Violation of subsection 1, paragraph A is a Class D crime; and violation of subsection 1, paragraph C is a Class E crime; except that the sentencing class for a violation of subsection 1 is one class higher if the state pleads and proves:

A. The actor was more than 10 years older than the other person; or

B. The actor knew the other person was related to the actor within the 2nd degree of consanguinity. *(Maine Statutes 17A §254. Sexual abuse of minors.)*

Regardless of the precise requirements for a criminal prosecution, healthcare providers who have reason to believe a minor child has been abused, sexually or non-sexually, are legally bound, in some states, to report the abuse to child protective authorities. A legal requirement to report child abuse relieves the clinician of legal risk of a lawsuit from parents if the clinician's suspicion is without merit. It does not relieve clinicians who worry about offending or traumatizing parents or upsetting the child. In states where reporting is not required, clinicians must use their professional judgment and weigh the strength of the data which supports a finding of abuse against the likelihood that injuries were caused by normal childhood accidents.

Involving Elderly Patients—In some states, the requirement to report abuse applies to the elderly as well as to minors.

Involving Competent Adults—For adult women, the burden of reporting sexual abuse falls on the patient. A clinician certainly can invite a patient to discuss any concerns regarding present or past sexual abuse and encourage the patient to report sexual assault. It is helpful for clinicians to know the basics of the legal process which begins after an individual has reported sexual abuse.

The legal process which takes place when a sexual abuse is reported is:

1. A police officer takes a report from the victim, including the specifics of the incident and the abuser's identifying information.

2. If the abuse has taken place in the past 24 hours, police may arrange for a clinician to conduct an examination of the victim looking for evidence of abuse. This may involve taking samples of residue from the patient's body areas which were involved in the incident—for

the purposes of DNA testing; and examination for bruises or lacerations. If the abuse was more than 24 hours in the past, police officers will have less interest in collecting physical evidence.

3. A police officer will interview the individual the victim has identified as the abuser.

4. Police officers will interview any individuals who were witnesses to the abuse.

5. Police officers will turn the evidence over to the local District Attorney's office, and prosecuting attorneys will decide whether to charge the individual the victim has named as the abuser.

6. If the named abuser is charged, the individual will be arrested. In some cases, prosecutors determine that the evidence is not strong enough to charge the named abuser.

For the victim, the process of giving an interview to police, detailing the incident of abuse, and possibly undergoing a physical examination for evidence is stressful. To undergo that process and then have a prosecutor decline to press charges is a further stressor. Some victims are fearful of naming an abuser and then having no charges brought. Some victims are fearful that the incident will become public knowledge. Some patients decline to report sexual abuse because they do not want to subject themselves to the legal process.

A clinician can try to help a victim of abuse in making a decision about whether, and when, to report an incident of abuse.

Domestic Violence

A 1993 survey of reported domestic violence in Maryland revealed the following:

- In 70% of cases, victims were current spouses

or had a child in common with the batterer.

- Incidents were most likely to occur between 6 PM and 3 AM.

- Incidents were most likely to occur on Friday, Saturday, or Sunday.

- 82.7% of spousal assault victims were female.

- Spousal assaults were 22.5% of the 86,591 assaults reported that year.

- 53.2% of the victims were white; 45.7% of the victims were African-American.

- Most often, victims were 25-40 years old.

- 73 victims died as a result of domestic violence.

(Source: Elgin SC. Domestic violence: Is Maryland responding? The Maryland Bar Journal. March-April 1995; 29(2):42.)

This data is based on reported cases of domestic violence. Researchers estimate that only 10% of domestic violence is reported.

Each state treats domestic violence differently. Domestic abuse may be defined by state law and may include battery; assault and battery; serious bodily injury; threat of injury, rape or sexual offense; attempted rape or sexual offense; imprisonment; abuse of a child or vulnerable adult; or mental injury to a child as verified by two physicians or social workers.

In some states, laws provide quick action for victims of domestic violence and quick remedies. In Maryland, for example, the following individuals might bring action against an abuser: the abuser's current or former spouse; a cohabitant; a person related by blood or marriage to the abuser, if they resided for at least 90 days in the year before relief is sought; a vulnerable adult; or an adult who has a child in common with the abuser.

Among the states that have domestic violence laws are Illinois, Kentucky, Ohio, New Jersey, New York, North Carolina, and the District of Columbia.

Under Maryland's law on domestic violence, a victim may report an incident to the District Court and get a hearing before a judge the next day. At the initial hearing, which is *ex parte* (without input from the accused), the victim tells the judge what happened, and the judge may choose among several short-term remedies. The remedies may include a restraining order which will order an individual to refrain from contacting the victim; maintain a specific distance from the victim, the victim's home, or employment; and refrain from further abuse. A victim who has a court order against the abuser may call police if the abuser violates the order, and the police will jail the abuser.

A hearing is set for a date within five days of the abuse. The alleged abuser and the abused, represented by attorneys, tell their stories to a judge. The judge may extend the restraining order, may order the abuser to pay the abused a living allowance and/or child support, and/or may award the house and/or car to the abused. The remedies may extend for up to 200 days.

Clinicians may help victims of domestic violence in the following ways:

1. Become familiar with the state law addressing domestic violence. It is not a clinician's job to offer legal advice. However, if a clinician suspects that a patient has been abused at home, part of the clinician's intervention could include educating the patient about the state's resources for victims. A telephone number for the appropriate state agency, given to a patient in need, can be a valuable healthcare service.

2. Become familiar with local resources for battered women, children, and vulnerable adults. Many communities have shelters for

battered women. All communities have child protective services, and most communities have adult protective services.

3. If there is physical evidence of trauma, such as bruises or lacerations, advise the victim to document the evidence in a photograph.

4. Become familiar with state law addressing the reporting of suspected abuse. If clinicians are legally required to report abuse, the clinician should advise the patient that the clinician has a duty to report the abuse.

5. Assist the victim in making a plan for ensuring a safe living situation for the next 24 hours—and for the long-term.

6. Treat the injuries.

7. Refer the patient for counseling, or conduct the counseling to the extent you are capable.

8. Make assessment for domestic abuse a part of the history-taking. Routine questions might include:

Are you safe at home?
Are your children safe at home?
Has anyone been hitting you?
Are you afraid of anyone you live with?

Domestic Violence Help "Hotlines"

The National Domestic Violence Hotline provides callers with crisis intervention, information about domestic violence, and referrals to local programs 24 hours a day, every day, in English and in Spanish. Interpreters are available to translate 139 languages. The service reports a volume of about 10,000 calls each month.

The number is 1-800-799-SAFE or from a TDD at 1-800-787-3224.

---

9. Plan interventions when the answers to the questions indicate that the patient is being abused. Women should have an escape plan if abuse has occurred in the past.

Substance Abuse During Pregnancy

A woman who is assessed at the time of childbirth as being under the influence of alcohol or drugs may lose her newborn to child protective services. In some states, the woman may be prosecuted for child neglect for activities undertaken while a child was *in utero*. On the other hand, pregnant women who are addicted to drugs or alcohol but who voluntarily enroll in a rehabilitation program while pregnant are at lower risk for loss of parental rights.

In South Carolina, a woman was convicted and sentenced to eight years in jail for using drugs during her pregnancy, even though her child was born healthy. In 1996, the state Supreme Court upheld the conviction.

While drug abuse during pregnancy is tragic, laws that call for criminal prosecution of pregnant women for endangering the lives of their fetuses are troublesome because of the gray areas inherent in the issue. For example, what is drug abuse? Does it include drinking wine with dinner? Smoking? Taking aspirin while pregnant? Could neglect of fetal rights be expanded to include a requirement that pregnant women take their prenatal vitamins or risk jail?

Clinicians caring for substance abusing pregnant women can advise the patient that she may be endangering her baby, that she is risking loss of parental rights if the baby is born addicted to drugs, and that there are programs open to pregnant women. However, a clinician who threatens to report the patient to child protective services is not likely to find that the patient will return for further prenatal visits.

Date Rape

Approximately 85% of rape victims are raped by someone they know. The picture of the rapist as a stranger who jumps out of the bushes is not consistent with the data.

In many states, the law addressing rape has not kept pace with the growing recognition that non-consensual intercourse often occurs without evidence of severe bodily harm.

The common law definition of rape is "carnal knowledge of a female, other than one's wife, by force or threat of force, and against her will." In many states, courts will require actual physical resistance by the victim and substantial force by the assailant as proof that intercourse was non-consensual. If the victim claims "threat of force," the courts will be looking for evidence that the rapist had a weapon.

In acquaintance rape, or date rape, it is the threat of force, rather than actual force, that is the focus. A victim who claims that intercourse occurred as a result of a threat of force might be required to show that she was placed in real apprehension of imminent serious bodily harm and that the fear was reasonable under the circumstances. In deciding whether the victim's fear was reasonable, a judge will consider the respective ages, the physical sizes, and the mental condition of the victim and accused.

The required degree of resistance of the victim varies from state to state. One of the most progressive states in terms of rape law is Washington. Washington has a third-degree rape statute, in addition to first- and second-degree rape. The third-degree rape statute criminalizes non-consensual intercourse without any show of force. Verbal resistance satisfies the legal requirement of resistance by the victim. *(Washington Revised Code Annotated §9A.44.060.)*

Victims are sometimes ambivalent about bringing charges. Young women often are reluctant to "ruin his life" by reporting a date or acquaintance rape. Victims may be unclear about how the situation evolved into rape, and whether they could have avoided the rape by protesting more assertively.

Clinicians should initiate discussions with young women about their right to consent or refuse sexual advances, how to decline sexual advances, how to avoid situations where rape might occur, and the related issues of the dangers of alcohol and drugs. Young women should understand that incidents often happen when one or both parties have been drinking alcohol. Young women should know that when a female who has been drinking alcohol brings a charge of date rape, the defense is likely to state that she was inebriated and unable to be clear about what happened, or that she consented, or that she failed to resist.

The best thing a clinician can do for patients is to teach them how to avoid date or acquaintance rape. Women and teenagers may be inexperienced with dating and sexual relationships and may be unclear about what is acceptable and unacceptable behavior.

Statutory Rape

In general, statutory rape is intercourse with an underage person. A child is presumed to be unable to give consent to intercourse. Each state defines statutory rape. For example, Missouri's definition is:

> *A person commits the crime of statutory rape in the second degree if being twenty-one years of age or older, he has sexual intercourse with another person who is less than seventeen years of age. Statutory rape in the second degree is a class C felony. (Missouri Revised Statutes, Chapter 566, Sexual Offenses, Section 566.034.)*

State definitions vary widely.

There are no data on the age of the partners of teenaged women. There are data on the ages of the fathers of children born to teenaged mothers. A 1995 study published by The Alan Guttmacher Institute reported that at least half of all babies born to minor women are fathered by adult men.

One issue being debated among policy-makers is whether enforcement of statutory rape laws would decrease sex among teenagers.

While it is not a clinician's job to police sex among teenagers, clinicians should know the age of consent in their state and should consider counseling sexually active teenagers that they are risking criminal prosecution, in addition to the other risks of sexual activity.

Additional Resources

Among additional sources of information on these legal topics are:

- The Internet
- Young Women's Christian Association (YWCA)
- Women's shelters and women's centers
- Sexual assault crisis centers and rape crisis center
- Hotlines

Please also see the list of health-related hotlines on page 120.

The author of this chapter, Carolyn Buppert, JD, CRNP, is an attorney specializing in healthcare issues and a practicing NP in the Baltimore, MD area.

APPENDIX A

SELECTED NATIONAL HEALTH HOTLINES

The following toll-free numbers provide health-related information. These organizations do not diagnose or recommend treatment for any disease. Some numbers offer recorded information, and others provide personalized counseling referrals and/or written materials. Unless otherwise stated, members can be reached within the continental U.S., Monday through Friday. Hours of operation are Eastern Time. Numbers that operate 24 hours a day can be reached seven days a week, unless otherwise noted. Numbers designated "TDD" are accessible to hearing-impaired people using a telecommunications device for the deaf. Phone numbers are subject to change without notice.

AIDS/HIV

National AIDS Hotline
1-800-342-2437

Spanish
1-800-344-7432

TDD
1-800-243-7889

Project Inform Hotline
1-800-822-7422

ALCOHOLISM

AJ-Anon Family Group Headquarters
1-800-356-9996

American Council on Alcoholism
1-800-527-5344

CHILDREN'S SERVICES

National Association for the Education of Young People
1-800-424-2460

National Child Abuse Hotline
1-800-422-4453

National Child Safety Council Childwatch
1-800-222-1464

National Clearinghouse on Family Support and Children's Mental Health
1-800-628-1696

DOMESTIC VIOLENCE

National Resource Center on Domestic Violence
1-800-537-2238

DRUG ABUSE

National Council on Alcoholism and Drug Dependence
1-800-622-2255

Workplace Helpline
1-800-843-4971

SEXUALLY TRANSMITTED DISEASES

National STD Hotline
1-800-227-8922